IS ANYONE
UP THERE?

IS ANYONE UP THERE?

How I Discovered God Loves the
Saved, the Unsaved, and Me

CINDI McCANN

Xulon Press

Xulon Press
2301 Lucien Way #415
Maitland, FL 32751
407.339.4217
www.xulonpress.com

Unless otherwise indicated, Scripture quotations taken from the HOLY BIBLE, New International Version (NIV). Copyright © 1973, 1978, 1984, 2011 by Biblica, Inc.™. Used by permission. All rights reserved.

Scripture quotations taken from the Good News Translation (GNT). Copyright © 1992 American Bible Society. Used by permission. All rights reserved.

Printed in the United States of America.

Author's Coach: Jacqueline Arnold, www.sweetlifeusa.com

ISBN-13: 9781545628034

DEDICATION

This book is dedicated to the most important people in my life. To my late father, Don Martin, who made me laugh and showed me what hard work and dedication can bring forth. To my Mom, Linda, who knows no stranger, and would gladly feed the world over and over. To my Husband Tom, thank you for letting me be me, and, to my beloved son, Jacob, without you in my life I would probably never had written my story, or become the person I am today. It would go without saying, to my sis Jill, the director and friend for life, and to my step sons, Thomas and John. Thank you for being who I 'always wanted to be when I grow up'.

ACKNOWLEDGEMENT

It would go without saying that none of this would have been possible without God. I am blessed that He chose me even before I chose Him.

You did not choose me, but I chose you and appointed you so that you might go and bear fruit—fruit that will last—and so that whatever you ask in my name the Father will give you. -John 15:16

Had Jesus not intervened in my life at the right time and place, I shudder to think where I would be. To the Sweet Holy Spirit who has lead me, comforted me and showed me how to love, I am deeply touched and grateful, for without the trinity, none of these words would have been written.

I would also like to give a special shout out to my dearest crazy evangelical friend, Lillian, and her husband Charles, who continually prayed for me and my family, and still do today. I also appreciate the countless hours I called and the patience with which they answered my questions, no matter the subject. To my sweet friend Vera, who encouraged me to write, and led me to find my Author's Coach, Jacqueline Arnold, who was instrumental in coaching me through writing this exciting book.

Special thanks go out to the countless people I have been involved with through Bible Studies, Mom's group, and Stephen Ministry, as well as the many others I worked with, both in the air and on the ground.

Each of one you have touched my life, been a part of my journey, and are a piece of my story. Thank you for all you encouraged in me - to be who God truly made me.

TABLE OF CONTENTS

INTRODUCTION

When you look up at the stars, what do you see? Perhaps, you are one who has taken astronomy and can call out all the constellations and each star by name. I am not such a person. I do, however, enjoy looking at the stars. When my son was younger, among our favorite things to do was stargazing. We loved watching the clouds moving through the bright blue sky. We would spot one and quickly call out the pictures the clouds formed. At that time, I never stopped to wonder, 'Is Anyone Up There?' – have you?

During that time, I just loved being a mom, and cherished my time with my son, enjoying his childhood, at Disney, or daydreaming under the clouds; all those tiny little things that add up to create a childhood.

My son was young, so many of his pictures were taken with Disney characters and all things Power Rangers. I was busy being a mom, caught up in the day-to-day of life. I didn't stop to think what things had impacted my faith and beliefs, and what things were guiding me as a mother?

I remember taking Greek Mythology in college and the professor would tell how each of the stars was a representation of some sort of mythological story of a Greek

God. Could you imagine living during those ancient times in Greece?

You had a God for fire, a God for food, a God for fertility and a God for health. What a confusing philosophy, and how tiresome for followers, rushing from God to God. I would be most confused to say the very least.

Just picture this - your husband comes home from working the fields, covered in dirt and with calluses on his hands, and he says, "Looks like we are going to need a miracle, the corn ears are small and we will not have enough to take to market."

You're thinking *this might not be the time to ask about purchasing a new rug for the living room floor,* as you had intended to present to him, instead, you suggest a trip to the temple to pray to the harvest God, and, instead of praying to the harvest God for good corn, you end up praying to the fertility God - and end up with twins.

I have often wondered if God can really hear me - or for that matter anyone. Who, if anyone, even calls upon the name of 'God?'

Fear not, I am not a monk, a Buddhist, or a 'super Christian' who knows all the answers, however, I am a person who likes to ask questions, and I'm even more thrilled when I get a response.

I would like to take you on a journey, full of questions and exploration to the depths of my inner soul. You see, I believe everyone in one point in their life will ask for a very definite answer to some deep, tough questions - the very poignant questions, such as, "Is God really there?" and, "Can God Actually Hear Me?"

This happened for me.

One day, I reached that point where I was ready to dig deep and discover for myself the real answers.

"Hello! God, are you there," I called out into what seemed like thin air.

I always knew He was, but not in a way that I was willing or ready to acknowledge Him, and even if He was, I thought, certainly, He didn't see me – or, hear me, or really love me.

Through my journey, I was able to uncover the answers to these mysteries. I was finally able to discover that God truly is – the Great I am; that God truly does see - and, He sees me, and, truly loves me – all through my lifetime, both when I was unsaved, and now that I am saved. I know for certain, God is truly 'up there.'

My son has now reached his teen years and cloud gazing is no longer a popular hobby between us, however, when I look at the clouds now, I see more than just formations in the clouds and I am drawn to ponder God in new and meaningful ways.

My ever-lingering question, "Hello, are you up there?" is now an affirming, "Hello, God, I see you, and, I know I am loved."

If you will have an open mind and heart, I believe that together, we will gain a better understanding of who we are, and, perhaps a better understanding of who God is. Please, feel free to question, and even argue, with what you find out. I know I have, and probably will continue to, as long as I am alive.

Explore with me and read how I discovered that God is real, and how He loves both the saved and unsaved. May my story richly bless you and may you discover this truth for yourself.

Chapter One

WHERE IT ALL BEGAN

Hi, my name is Cindi McCann, and, like all good stories, it's best to start from the beginning. My humble beginnings are where it all began - the foundation of my life and my beliefs. I realize you cannot tell from my name, but my family background is Jewish. I was born in Des Plaines, IL, in a small suburb town, which was a community of mixed conservative and orthodox Jews.

My parents were born in New York, my dad from Long Island and my mom from the Bronx. During one summer of my father's youth, he went to an orthodox camp and decided he wanted to become a Rabbi. His parents were not happy with this idea and strongly encouraged him to attend New York University (NYU), and get a degree he could use later on in life. My father's dad was in the rag business and wanted him to continue the family tradition in textiles.

My mom's family came from modest means and her dad did not finish high school, but as they say back then, "an eighth- grade education is all you need in life." Her parents were not very religious. They were both very hard-working people with not a lot of tangible assets.

My mom grew up in a one-bedroom apartment, sleeping on a pull-out couch all of her life. My mom was very bright, and a great ballet dance. She attended Julliard, during where she met Penny Marshal and many other famous people.

Dad attended Yeshiva, an Orthodox Jewish school, or seminary, and, also NYU, and continued his religious studies, eventually receiving a degree in Business.

My father always had an inquisitive mind. While growing up, he and a friend decided to make cherry bombs in my dad's basement, and accidentally blew up the basement. My dad ran away from home for three days until his father had time to calm down; this was a theme for most of his life, not blowing things up, but trying new ideas.

My dad's cousin Magda, who is a Holocaust survivor from Poland, lived next door to my mom's parents. Magda told my mom's mother that she has a wonderful cousin who lives on Long Island and who would be 'a perfect match for your daughter.' My cousin Magda and my Mom's mother agreed it would be a good match, they went to the matchmaker and the rest is history.

When my parents first married, my father was a buyer for women's clothing. This was incredibly good fortune since at the time my Aunt Carol who was ten years my senior came to live with my parents. My Aunt Carol was not the brightest, or should I say, she was bright but most of her attention was on boys, not on her grades. You are probably asking yourself what's the connection? My dad was able to bribe the teachers with designer clothing to ensure my Aunt would pass in school.

My dad also loved working with his hands. You know the type; give him a broken whatever and he will fix it. My father was also brilliant. He built his own computer back in the early '80s. My father skipped two grades and said it was the biggest mistake his parents made. When asked why he said that, he answered, "I could not go out with any girl in high school, and the worst part of it was - the girl would have to drive because I was not old enough."

My father enjoyed working with his hands and decided to go back to school and get his license as a heating and air serviceman. Dad opened his own business after working for several other companies in the Heating and Air Conditioning business.

My mother started working for my Dad when I was in middle school. My Mom later went to work for the Greater Miami Jewish Federation until retirement. As a result, my father was asked by the Rabbi from Federation to work some of the cruise ships during the High Holidays. My father did everything, as he would say, "But marry them and bury them. "

My family line consisted of several generations of observant religious men. In fact, I was named after my mother's grandfather, and his name was Charlie. His Hebrew name was Chaim and my Hebrew name is Chia meaning Life. My father's side of the family came from Poland and Romania. My dad's family lost many of his uncles and aunts, along with extended members of his family, due to the holocaust. Both my parents could trace our family line to the tribe of Israel. The point I am making is that I was a confident Jew; my identity never wavered. I loved being Jewish, along with every aspect of the culture, history and religious practices. It was a part of my foundation.

During the harsh winters in Chicago, my mom had suffered several miscarriages and developed various health issues. The doctors suggested that we move to a warmer climate to ease my mom's suffering. So, dad decided to move to Florida, and we moved to Kendal, a new city in the developmental stages, in south Miami.

We all loved the climate change and we had the added bonus of a swimming pool in our backyard, which we happily used every day. Within about two months of moving, things changed in our lives.

We were part of a community and attended a Conservative Temple. Which meant we drove to temple, instead of walked, which is typical of members in conservative temples. We ate 'questionable foods' such as lobster and shrimp, which is strictly prohibited in the Jewish faith. My sister, Jill, who was older, thought this was the greatest thing ever and, as a result, her social circle was full.

On the other hand, most of my friends lived in the North Miami Beach area, a mix of conservative and orthodox community, and a distance only to be reached by car.

When the High Holiday festivities came, everyone from both sides of the family would come to our house. Our house was the hub, mainly because we lived in Florida and my Grandma Honey (my mom's mom), was the best cook. I remember one Passover looking over the table where everyone was sitting and laughing. I thought to myself how strange it was that they were sitting by country of origin instead of sitting next to their spouses.

My Dad called me over and asked, "What are you thinking?" I told him and he said, "you should hear what I am hearing. I think this is how the third world war will start."

The conversation was heated and lively at times. You see, it was normal for us to have at least 15 to 20 friends and relatives in the home to celebrate, in spite of the small space. I might add the house only had three bedrooms.

While attending high school, the school offered an exchange program to Israel. I worked and earned the funds to go. I was eager to go because I wanted to see where it all began. I think for my parents it was an opportunity for me to meet a nice Jewish boy. I loved it so much in Israel. I continued my studies by attending Tel Aviv University.

When I first arrived in Israel, Carter was president, and the Iran hostage's situation was just beginning. While in college, Reagan became president, and the war in Lebanon was in full swing.

I was excited to be studying in Israel, and just as my mom had hoped, I soon met a nice Israeli boy, also attending the university. He was working to become a doctor, and we quickly became engaged.

On our first vacation he took me to Eilat, the popular vacation capital for many. It was wonderful and looked just like the postcards or a scene from the movies. We swam in the Dead Sea, or should I say floated. That night we met up with other friends from the University and made a small bonfire.

As evening was approaching I asked my fiancé if it was a holiday.

"No, why?" he asked me, perplexed at my question.

I pointed up to the sky, "look up, there are fireworks going off."

Everyone stopped talking and my fiancé smiled, took my hand, and said, "No dear, those aren't fireworks, they are bombs going off from Lebanon." That was the first time it hit me that there was a war going on, yet everyone I was with was undisturbed, not terrified or bothered, like I was.

I stayed for three years when my mom begged me to come home and get an American degree. To be honest, I was tired of the sirens going off. The last straw was when

I was working for Bank Leumi as a secretary, and the bus taking me from Ramat Gan, the small town where I lived, to downtown Tel Aviv, had a bomb scare. There were two other buses that had been pulled into the station and everyone was running to evacuate. The bomb squad was there and the bus next to us blew up. Somehow, this did not disturb me; I accepted it as the norm. My parents had enough after that incident and insisted I come home, as well.

I returned home, without my fiancé, no longer engaged. Without going in to details, he was injured in the Lebanon War and needed medical care. I was unable to meet his need. I returned home, finishing my degree at a local community college.

While studying, my desire to travel and get back to Israel intensified, because I missed the country and the people there. A friend of mine from high school told me about an ad she saw in the paper. She said that Pan American Airways was hiring Stewardesses, and encouraged me to go for an interview, "this way you can travel all over the world, and get paid for it," she said. That was a no brainer. I went for an interview, was hired that day, and started training the following week. I worked for Pan Am until 1991, and was hired to Delta Airlines in time, where I worked from 1991 to 2008.

There were many interesting adventures and experiences while I was with Pan Am, and I will share many going forward, like the time Joel Osteen showed interest and asked me out on a date. Suffice it to say, that date never transpired, and God had another mate in mind for me.

I met my husband, Tom, during a missed flight to Miami, and then again during another flight, when he was captain of the flight I was also serving on. He was a gentleman, giving up his seat for me on our first meeting, and making light of a messy situation the next time we met in-flight. I know he was the right man for me when, during a sudden drop of elevation, I dropped the pilot's meals everywhere, and all over myself, and he said, "I like mine shaken, not stirred."

We married in 1994, at Disney World, under the Monorail, and, life was magical. We loved living in Orlando, FL. Eventually, we transferred to New York, due to his flight hub reassignment, and had remodeled what we called the 'Archie Bunker' house to make our house a home.

My pilot-husband switched aircrafts, along with bases, and, eventually, we flew south to our long-term home in Peachtree City, GA, with our teenage son, and our dog, Jack. Our family continues to grow, as my two step-sons are married to wonderful women now. The newest member of the McCann family is our grand-daughter Gladney Gray known as 'GG.'

Life is fantastic!

Chapter Two

HEARS BUT DOES NOT REALLY HEAR

When I was growing up, my family and I always attended Temple, or as my dad would say, with that thick New York accent, 'Shul.' As mentioned before, I was brought up Jewish. We belonged to a conservative synagogue (Temple). When we first arrived in Miami, FL, our congregation met in a bank building until we had enough funds to purchase a building and land.

I attended a school with a student body of mostly gentiles, and I might add the area I lived in Miami, was up and coming. People would find it very funny that the Temple was on top of a bank. I am sure you have heard all the stereotypes depicting Jewish people as 'tight with their money.' Then, you can use your imagination to the comments some people made of our location, especially those in school. The Rabbi would joke that we 'keep our money close to us.' Dad would say we have 'direct deposit to God and money.' In either case, we were at the bank for several years for Temple.

My father owned his own business installing and repairing air conditioners. Dad made a great income, because of his hard- work and dedication to our family, we enjoyed a nice life. One time, I recall my dad and mom won a trip to China, thanks to dad's hard- work and selling the most AC units.

My parents left for China and were gone for several weeks. My grandparents came to live with us and care for us at that time. I loved it! My grandmother never asked for help in the kitchen and gramps did almost all of our chores. In other words; we were spoiled rotten, and we loved it. The only task we had was to mow the lawn since gramps never did that in his life, and he said he was not about to at his age. I couldn't understand why gramps did not want to help with the grass; he was a human sundial. Gramps favorite thing was to lie outside every afternoon. He would say, "I am going to get my vitamin D shot," as he headed outside for a few minutes in the sun.

My parents came home from China with so many amazing artifacts and stories. The family favorite was the pachinko machine. It was basically a pinball machine without the use of electricity; it was hours of entertainment for everyone. We all got fans and clothes from China. Dad loved to tell the story of how American food was making its way into China. Mom shared a favorite story about when they were eating at a Chinese pizza parlor. "It was *very* funny," she said.

"How is that funny?" we all screamed. Mom said that the ladies were in their traditional kimonos, which have very long sleeves. They would roll up their sleeves and use chopsticks to eat their pizza. I could not see that in my mind. I asked dad if that was true? Dad being the comedian, got out chopsticks, and showed us how to eat pizza with them. He could not do it very well, and after the fourth time falling on the floor, we agreed, it was not only funny, it was hysterical. Mom said that when she and daddy walked into the pizza place and sat down everyone turned around and smiled. When the pizza arrived and they began to eat with their hands, everyone began to laugh, and, in return, when they saw how the local people ate their pizza with chopsticks, the other people in the restaurant laughed.

Dad said it was the most beautiful place he had ever been. He said that they have gardens like we have never seen. The closet thing we have ever seen of China, or its culture, is when we ate at Chinese restaurants. Zen gardens had not come to the states, or the beautiful Asian landscaping. My dad was completely inspired, and insanely passionate, with having a Chinese garden of his own.

After sharing the details of their trip, Dad announced in his typical manner, "I have an *IDEA!*" We all looked at each other at the dinner table wondering who was going to be the assistant, as my mom began calculating cost of this grand idea. No one was expecting Dad to exclaim, "We should make our own Zen garden, including a waterfall and stream and, even a koi pond with fish!"

Mom asked where exactly he planned to put this wonderful idea.

"Come with me," Dad said with certainty, as he took my mom's hand and led us all outside with pomp and circumstance. Dad was already prepared to outline his idea and had a spray can of paint in his hand, and began to spray the entire backyard to demonstrate his vision.

We were all stunned. Mom calmly asked him how he planned to actually install such a ginormous pond, to which he replied with a serious tone, "I'm not sure, but, I will figure it out at the right time."

It took a while for him complete it, but all of us were very excited to watch the pond unfold. We had an acre of yard that nobody used, except for the dogs. Mostly, we stayed in the enclosed screened-in pool area and didn't venture out to the lawn. The pool area housed a massive entertainment area. It was fully equipped with everything we could possibly want – we didn't need to venture out to the grassy area. My dad had put in a bar, dining area, and poolside lounging area. It was the best house to grow up in!

The next week my dad came home with a bulldozer - that was mind blowing. My grandparents came for their weekly visit and both of them said, "Linda, you better call the hospital." Mom asked dad if he knew what he was doing. His favorite line was, "I asked a guy," as if this was the answer to all things. Dad did great operating the bulldozer, the only problem was that we lived in Florida, our sub ground was coral rock, and nothing was going to penetrate that bed of natural rock.

Our next -door neighbor was an older couple with five kids ranging in age from newborn to fifteen. The wife worked as a nurse, the husband stayed home with the kids - and just happened to be a retired military veteran with demolition experience.

I might add our other neighbor was a cop who had friends from the bomb squad. What could go wrong, right? They're all professionals, right?

As dad began to work on the project, the entire neighborhood gathered to watch. People came with their lawn chairs and coolers, watching my dad and his buddies as sideline cheerleaders. One such time was when the bulldozer could not go any further to penetrate the coral bed, and began to smoke. One neighbor yelled out, "Should I call the fire department?"

Another asked if we should call the hospital. That is when the most surprising thing happened. Our next-door neighbor, the military explosives expert, came over and offers strategic advice. My dad's face lit up, and the two of them came up with a plan to -basically blow up the backyard. My mom's screaming, "No, DONALD!" Mom was using his full name, and we all know that this means, war!"

My dad screams back, "LINDA, he's an expert! Nothing is going to go wrong! He's the guy!"

My mom tells us girls and everyone else to back up. It was watching a herd of cattle being moved in unison. Before anyone could call the fire department, or the hospital, this loud boom penetrated the air! Everything that was on the ground was flying haphazardly through the air. Every boy in the neighborhood thought my dad was the coolest dad, and every woman thought 'that poor woman has to live with THAT man.'

I have to admit that it was crazy, and, after the third time it worked, and no one went to the hospital. Simultaneously, we also got a well, which everyone enjoyed.

It took the help of the entire family working together full time to put this grand vision together. It was almost finished, when my dad decided we needed koi in the pond. The pond was mostly inhabited by frogs at this point, and all the dogs used it to drink out of. He reached out to one of his clients who owned a Chinese food restaurant. The owner of the restaurant told my dad he could have ten koi for his new pond. Dad went and caught seven koi and brought them home to our pond. After several months, the koi must have enjoyed living in our backyard, because we soon had fifteen. It was a good thing he didn't come home with ten, or we would have had a full school!

It was amazing to have it completed, and it looked great. Everyone in the neighborhood would come over to look and, I might add, it was pretty enough, we had a few weddings there, too. But, it cost a lot. I am not just talking financially, but, mentally and socially. My dad became consumed with this project; he was constantly researching which plants to plant and where to plant them. Dad went completely overboard, everyone was feeling it, even me.

I will never forget this one event, it had rained, as it always does in sunny Florida, but this time it was a gully washer. We got so much rain that the koi pond had overflowed and the koi were out of the pond and lying in the grass.

"Here goes another Saturday dedicated to dad's project," I said under my breath.

I cannot tell you how many parties, movies and times hanging out with friends that were missed, all for that garden. There was dad, screaming for everyone to "wake up, the koi are dying in the yard," -just what every teen wants to do on a Saturday - go out in the pouring rain and try to catch koi in the middle of a squall. No one was happy.

The following week I tried to tell dad how unhappy I was, that I did not have any time to be with friends and do normal kid things. Dad had other plans going on in his head than listening to me that was evident when he would say, "What do you think about this now?" I felt frustrated.

It was Friday night and we all were heading for synagogue. We sang our usual songs, and then the rabbi began with the reading of the Torah (Bible), from Isaiah 42:20.

Hears but does not really hear.

I had asked God, "What is wrong with me that my dad can't understand me?" Then I heard this soft, gentle voice say, 'hears but does not really hear;' reminding me of the scripture that was just said.

Wow! I looked around, and asked my mom if she heard that, and she shook her head no, and asked me to stop turning around.

Did I just hear from God, I wondered? The service continued and I never doubted that was indeed God telling me something. I had forgotten all about that until I had that conversation with Him years later. Could God be talking to me?

Chapter Three

MIND READER

M y mother was involved with a Jewish organization called Organization for Rehabilitation Training (ORT). ORT began in Russia in 1880 to help impoverished Jews to acquire skills that would enable them to become self-sufficient.

During the remarkable course of 135 years, spanning revolutions and wars, ORT has endured, and grown, through its ability to adapt to change. Today, ORT provides skills-training and self-help projects throughout the world, using funds raised by its supporters, and matched by development agencies and national governments, to assist people on a path to economic independence.

My mom started as a member, became chapter treasurer, and later president. At one of her meetings, they had an entertainer who did tarot card readings. My mom came home with the tarot cards and sat my sister Jill and me down at the kitchen table to get a closer look. My mom told us to pick four cards and memorize them. We did and placed the cards face down in front of us. My mom asked my sister to tell her what cards I had. My sister got all four cards right the first time. It was then my turn. I could not even name one of them. I demanded we try again. So, we went back to the deck and we each picked four cards. We were facing each other with cards close to our chest. Once we memorized them, we put the cards face down on the table. This time I was going to go first, but I still could not name one, then my sister takes her turn again and she gets them all correct. My mom could see I was getting frustrated, and she took the cards and threw them in the trash, saying she should have never brought these cards into the house.

That night the strangest thing happened. We all went to bed, but I could not sleep. I noticed the alarm clock indicating it was 1:00, then 2:00, then 3:00. I sat up, and there was this man standing in the corner of my room, almost like he was floating. I looked at him, and he smiled, and said to me, "would you like to have the same ability your sister has in reading cards?"

I was puzzled, but the man was very handsome, and I did not feel scared for some reason.

I thought about it for a minute and said, "No, it doesn't seem like fun."

"What would you like most of all, then?" he asked.

I thought about being a rock star with a great voice. The man said, "I can do that, and then he showed me how I would tour the world and people would want to be my friend."

Then this feeling inside of me began to stir and the man said, "All you have to do is get on your knees and worship me."

"Like God?" I asked.

"Exactly," he said, anticipating my agreement.

"Wouldn't that be wrong?" I asked.

"No, I love God, not you," I said. And, just like that, he was gone.

I have no doubt that the good-looking man standing in my room was Satan himself. That was when I realized that God was real and, so was the devil.

Years later, I learned that even though the cards were something appearing harmless, or so I thought, it had everlasting consequences. Perhaps, you did not play with cards, but, perhaps you played that game 'light as a feather.'

I know some people used Ouija boards as a source of entertainment and even innocently gave them as gifts; in either case, these games are not at all harmless. Like anything you do in life, there are consequences for your actions.

I was attending a bible study and we were studying "Bad Girls of the Bible," when the conversation came up about going to fortune tellers and mediums. In the study, King Saul had gone to a medium to ask the prophet Samuel what to do. The prophet scolded King Saul saying, "Why you have waked me from my slumber when you already know the answer?"

You see, Saul knew what the bible said about consulting mediums.

"If any of you go for advice to people who consult the spirits of the dead, I will turn against you and will no longer consider you one of my people."

Leviticus 20:6, Good News Translation (GNT)

Saul did not care what the consequence was he only wanted what he wanted. It turned out to be the demise of King Saul.

In my humblest opinion, I believe when we do such things, we are usurping God's authority. Maybe you don't believe in God but, there is always a good reason when in the bible it says not to do something, you just don't do it.

As I said before, we were in Bible study having this discussion about tarot cards and such when one of the moms says, "Look, if my daughter wants to do 'light as a feather,' I'm going to let her."

"You know now that the bible says don't do it."

"Yes," she agreed, "but, I don't see why it's a big deal."

I told her that might be great for you, but what about all those other kids who might think this is real and start getting into other cult things.

"My daughter is stronger than that," She said.

I tried to get her to see the Truth, "What of the other girls who are there, perhaps they are not, what about them?" At this point everyone stopped their conversation and wanted to know if we both were ok. We both screamed back, "Of course we are."

A few weeks later, the same woman who said she would allow her daughter and friends to play those games approached me, "I thought a lot about what you said, and you are right, it's not right for me to jeopardize someone else's safety, or worse to corrupt them in the wrong way."

I told her I understand things are different when you have children and it's difficult to take a stand, but, more importantly, instead of seeking and searching through things God finds offensive, she could explore His word and discover that he offers an alternative.

I shared with her about when I was working as a flight attendant on a layover and there were two women who were tarot card readers, and they asked if I would like to participate. I shook my head no, but the girl I was flying with said, "I'll go."

She returned fifteen minutes later. I was curious and asked her, "What did the card reader say?"

The girl looked like she was in shock and then nearly pushed me to go; too "you need to go!"

"Fine!" I said, giving in to her dramatic insisting.

I found the young woman and first asked her where does she get her power? The girl looks at me as if I had a third eye. She says no one has ever asked that of me. She says I believe in God, and I know I should not be doing this but, my sister and mom won't leave me alone because I have 'the gift.'

She throws the cards on the table, and she said, "Don't touch them, it will make you unclean."

I quickly pull my hand back, and she says, "I will pull cards for you."

Now I am freaked out, yet curious at the same time.

She looks to me and said, "The man you are engaged to, you will not marry."

Holy moly, I was not wearing my engagement ring because my fiancé was getting it sized. How did she even know I was engaged? My mouth was hanging wide open and she had more to say, "You will not get married until you are older."

I thought *how much older, I am almost twenty-eight?*

She went on to say I would be married twice, and that my second husband will be the love of my life. Well, she was right about one. I did not marry that guy that I was currently engaged to, and, yes, I married later in life, and am still very married.

Chapter Four

FLY AWAY

My career with Pan Am suddenly took off. I was hired, went to training the following week, and got based in New York just six weeks later. It was already showing signs of wonderful adventures ahead.

I began my career as a flight attendant with Pan Am in the early '80s. Anyone over the age of thirty will know about this company, I'm sure. At the time, Pan Am was the most recognized symbol in the world, just like Coke.

Pan Am was a world class airline. They flew everywhere you could ever want to go to from North to South, and, East to West.

When I first began my career, I was based in New York, commuting from Miami. I was raised in Miami from the time I was in third grade. All of my family and friends were in Miami. Pan Am did have a base in Miami, but the base was made up of National, another airline company that was bought out by Pan Am, so Miami was not my hub, plus the trips out of Miami were horrible, and were offered to very senior staff.

Just in case you are not familiar with the term 'senior,' it has nothing to do with how the person looks or how aged they are, rather how long they have been working for the company; it refers to their tenure.

When I first began my career with Pan Am, I took the flight schedule and began to systematically bid on trips of my most desired destinations. Although, I was too junior to hold great trips, I was always able to pick them up when someone backed out or got diverted. I have been everywhere from Africa to Zagreb. I was exposed to so many cultures that this book should be that of a travel guide to unexpected hidden treasures of the world you can discover when you travel.

My life experiences were nonexistence until my job with Pan Am; I lived a very quiet, sheltered, and boring life. Until I started flying, I never even knew or met someone that was 'gay' or lived an 'alternative' lifestyle. Pan Am opened my eyes to a whole 'nother realm. In fact, my first roommate was a homosexual male who loved to cross-dress - now that is a story, because I had never been exposed to such things.

I was flying to London when my trip got cancelled because of weather in London. I came back to my 'crash pad,' in-between housing for those working in the airline industry, only to find my roommate in my gold Lamaze dress (yes, this was the disco era). The worst part of the encounter was that he looked great in it, and I could never bring myself to wear it again - knowing he was 'commando' in my dress. (That is sans under garments!). Life lesson: never leave behind anything you don't want someone else to wear.

That was my introduction to cross-dressers, never would have known if I hadn't seen it with my own eyes. You're probably wondering what all this has to do with hearing from God. The story has absolutely nothing, and yet, everything.

I should start from the beginning so there won't be any confusion.

My first trip to India was full of first educational lesson on life for me. I met this really nice local girl who worked the ground support for Pan Am and asked me if I wanted to go shopping. What woman would refuse such an opportunity like that?

First, we had lunch. This was my first experience with going out with locals. I smiled, as she ordered in her native language, and, then, I said I will have the same and smiled.

BIG mistake! I was not familiar with fire hot foods. I still can smell the burning sensation in my nostrils as I inhaled when they brought out the food, I might add I could not identify whether I was eating animal or vegetable. At one point I could not feel my lips and tongue; this went on for some time.

The girl laughed and suggested I get some milk.

"Good idea, I will." I agreed, fanning my lips.

For those of you not familiar with India, the cow is sacred, so no cow's milk is available, just goat's milk or other, whatever that source is! The milk arrived in a large glass. I slammed it down to quickly to cool my burning lips.

"YUCK!" I nearly spit it out toward the end, and it was warm, making it even more unappealing. We shared a good laugh about that. Well, more like she laughed, and I tried to cover up my swollen lips and my bruised pride!

India is also where I got my first parasite, as I like to loving call it, my 'Delhi Belly'. To this day, I get 'Delhi Belly' right before Christmas. Every doctor has tried to kill this parasite but with no success. The parasite stays dormant and comes out just in time for the holidays.

As we finished our meal, my friend says, "Let's go, and get our henna on."

Why not, I thought? It was first placed on my feet, *no problem*. I reason with myself, *I'll just wear black pantyhose; no one will see.*

That henna lasted *three months*. It was very interesting because my next trip was to Rio and I had to continually explain to people that I did not have a rash, which was very comical. It wasn't really a laughing matter; visible tattoos were grounds for termination. I was taking a big risk.

After our henna treatments, we went to the marketplace. My eyes were coming out of their sockets. It's like taking Walmart and Nordstrom and putting them on steroids, at the same time. We would walk the aisles and I would tell her, "I like that one," as I would point to the one item or garment I liked. She grabbed my hands, which were pointing to every other item on display, and she asked, "didn't your mother show you anything?"

I felt like answering her with the truth, and saying my mother has never heard 'attention Kmart shoppers,' or that it's possible to go shopping to a place that does not have valet parking. This is how I was raised; you see it and buy it. No, No, that is not how they do things in India or anywhere in the world, for that matter.

Lesson one she says "you never tell them that you like it, they will raise the price quickly, and never accept the first offer for the price." Clearly this woman must have read Trump's book, *The Art of the Deal*.

The thing that is most fascinating about India is the vast amount of people. No matter where your eyes go, there is always a crowd. In India, there are many people and many different religions, too. I found out that this is the mecca for all religions. To be honest, I had no idea that there were so many different religions or 'cults,' as my husband would say. Even in the religion of Hinduism there are several sects. India is home to at

least nine recognized religions. The major religions prac-
ticed in India are Hinduism, Islam, Christianity, Sikhism,
Buddhism and Jainism; Zoroastrianism, Judaism and the
Baha'i Faith are also practiced in India.

On a brighter note, I did get to meet Mother Teresa
while in India. Remember it's the early '80s; she had not
yet been spotlighted in the news. This was an amazing
time for me. I had been flying for less than a year, and to
be honest, I did not know she was a person of celebrity.
Mother Teresa was sitting in a business class seat, and,
she was very tiny. At first, I did not see her, and nearly
pushed the seat on top of her from behind trying to get
my bag out from under the seat. When I realized she was
sitting there, I pushed the seat back and was in tears apol-
ogizing to her.

She smiled and very meekly said, "It is okay."

One of the flight attendants told me who 'the nun'
was and joked, "You are definitely going to hell now!"

Needless to say, I felt terrible. I went up to her during
the flight to express my remorse. She said she was fine
and not to worry. I told her that I keep a book of all the
movie stars, political leaders and mover and shakers of
the time, and asked her if she would sign the book, or if
she could share with me a takeaway for life. She asked me
if I was a Christian. I politely told her "No, I am Jewish."

She smiled and said, "I will pray for you."

"It's nice to be nice," she smiled her toothy grin,
sharing with me her takeaway for life. To this day, I share
that morsel of wisdom with every child and adult I meet,
and it has made a lasting impression on all of us; the nice
seed has been planted.

While commuting from Miami to New York I met this
crazy Evangelical flight attendant named Lillian. Lillian
would talk to me all the time about God and how much
her life was better that she had Jesus in it. I would politely

smile or pretend I was sleeping if she and I had to sit next to each other on the airplane or jump seat. Lillian would say to me that I should 'try Jesus;' I would politely tell her that Jews are like the 'original recipe,' referring to Kentucky Fried Chicken, and Christians are like the 'extra crispy,' it may taste better, but the original was better for you. She would laugh and tell me, "God wants to hear from you." To which I would reply, "God is too busy to listen to me, but I know He is there."

Lillian always had her bible open, reading it and smiling all the time. Then the inevitable happened - we worked together. It was a horrible trip. In fact, we encountered some of the worst turbulence ever experienced in my career.

This was the turbulence where you hear screaming, followed by the deafening silence. As I looked over at Lillian, she was smiling and singing, she had this calmness about her. I looked over at her, and asked her if she was on drugs; she laughed, and said, "No."

As soon as the turbulence subsided, I asked, "How is it possible to be so calm?" "I have Jesus!" she exclaimed.

She slid closer to me on the jump seat, as if to tell me the greatest secret ever shared, and she began to share her testimony.

Lillian shared with me that she was raised Catholic, had a child out of wedlock, was excommunicated from her church, and, as a result, rejected by her family.

"I don't understand how this is a good thing," I said, baffled, "that sounds horrible."

She confided to me how she was afraid in her situation, fearful of losing her job, and not sure how to bring this child into the world, especially since her then boyfriend and father of the child wanted nothing to do with the baby.

Lillian was under tremendous stress. But you would never know she had anything going on beneath her smile and soft singing. She believed that God had a plan for her and her son.

I sat there amazed and astonished. Lillian told me that she wasn't always this way. Lillian said she met this flight attendant in New York who told her about having a personal relationship with Jesus Christ. Lillian said that the flight attendant made it sound like Jesus was right there with her always. Lillian explained that she was eager to enjoy the same relationship, and that she said the sinner's prayer, and began to read her bible that the flight attendant gave her, as a result.

Lillian had many questions, this flight attendant told her about a couple based in Miami who also worked for Pan Am, and that she should talk with them, and possibly attend church with them. Lillian contacted the couple and they became her mentors and friends and are still to this very day.

Thereafter, whenever I would see Lillian she would say to me "ALL THE TIME! No matter the problem, just talk to God."

I would always say back, "God is too busy to listen to me - who am I?"

After all of this exchange, Lillian would smile and say, "God loves you."

This went on for years….

As a flight attendant, we have mailboxes for intercompany mail, and as a place to drop notes to our colleagues. I would often find my box full of these leaflets, which I later learned were called 'tracts,' about Jesus. I knew they were from Lillian, and I would use them to write notes on, or put them into other people's boxes that I either did not care for or who I thought 'needed them more than me.'

On one of my flights I was schedule to work a charter flight from Texas to Paris, then continuing on to Israel. It was a packed flight. The flight consisted of people wearing black badges.

One of the crew members I was flying with said "look, those people are like the ones that come to your home and tell you about Jesus!"

Another flight attendant said, "I think they are called Jehovah Witness."

"What is that?" I asked.

The one flight attendant who started the conversation said, "My mom says to stay away from 'those people' with the black badges, they are like a cult - you know, like Jim Jones, and don't believe in the true Jesus!"

The other flight attendant looked scared, which scared me.

I was the most junior attendant on this flight, which meant I had to push pull carts while everyone else had a partner to work with.

As I began the service, this young man says to me, "Do you mind?" indicating for me to move the push cart out of the aisle. "I need to use the restroom."

I let out a huff and pushed both carts back to give him access. Just as I began the service again, he finished and needed access to the aisle, back to his seat.

From behind me, I heard, "Sorry, finished," to which I replied, "Did you flush?" and he quickly replied, "Yes, and washed my hands," as he raised both hands for me to inspect. We both laughed.

"Can I help you?" he quickly offered.

I dismissed his offer and replied with a dismissive, "Thank you, but sit down and enjoy being spoiled."

As we finished the first service, we were already preparing for the second cabin service. That same young man came up to me and introduced himself as Joel Osteen, and boldly asked me for my name in return.

We had a short conversation, and I did share my name. Not a minute later, I notice that there is a special meal for me to deliver to a passenger.

"Dodie Osteen?" I called out.

Yet again, Joel called out to me, "Hey, that's my mom!"

I moved toward her seat to deliver her meal and started chatting with Joel on the way over; he was not sitting near his mom.

"I love your mom's name, Dodie," I said to him as I made my way with her food tray. "Does she know what it means in Hebrew?"

"I don't know," Joel answered.

I tell him I'm going to tell her when I deliver her food tray. Off I go, with Joel following right behind me.

I approached Ms. Dodie and said, "Your name is my favorite Hebrew name, and do you know what it means in Hebrew?"

She smiled and said, "Yes."

I gushed, "If I have a child, I would name her Dodie; it means beloved."

Ms. Dodie asks with a smile, "Are you a believer?"

"I believe in God, and, yes, I am Jewish," I responded, but rather taken aback I was even being asked.

She smiled, and asked, "Would you ever think of converting to Christianity?"

I looked at her with such unbelief. How can anyone ask a Jew this? I smiled as hard as I could and very firmly said, "No."

In my mind and in my heart, this was very hurtful, and downright offensive. Then, Ms. Dodie added, "I will pray for you that God would reveal Himself to you."

"Thanks," I said with all the enthusiasm I could muster.

Little did I know that her words would haunt me for years? Whenever I had doubts about life and God, I would hear Ms. Dodie's voice in my head, thinking that God was going to reveal Himself to me. I would pause and ask myself, *do I want this?* After all, most people that experience God in such a way usually don't live long after the encounter, look at those who touched the Tabernacle or the Arc of the Covenant - Dead. I know I was not worthy to be in His presence. And, death didn't sound very appealing – just yet.

On a side note, after eventually accepting Christ into my life, I did not immediately remember my encounter with Joel on that flight. It was not until my husband and I moved from New York to Atlanta when I began to watch TBN on a regular basis that the meeting came to my remembrance.

I saw Joel on the television but did not remember or recognize him from that significant flight. However, when he started speaking about his mother Dodie and how she overcame cancer, and the camera moved to her and showed her face, it was quite telling. I remembered her with intensity, and I dropped the remote. I have no doubt in my mind a seed was planted by Dodie during that flight, and I was jarred that night I saw her again on television. Thank you, Ms. Dodie, I love you!!!!

Chapter Five

INTO THE LIGHT

My life was great - I had a great job that I loved, travelled the world, went to places people read about or dream about; it was all I had dreamed. The people were just as interesting as well. I met kings, princes, and princesses, heads of government, movie stars, rock stars, entrepreneurs, and people who were going places.

I shopped around the world for treasures for a house that I had just purchased, not to mention found just the right new car. Life was exciting, glamorous, and downright fun.

I remember I was flying from Miami to New York and I ran into a friend from high school who had graduated from Harvard as an attorney, her long- life dream, not to mention she was sitting with her husband, also graduated from Harvard, as an attorney.

We started talking about our lives. I told her how I was impressed with her attending Harvard, and now a big shot lawyer in New York, with a handsome husband to boot. She smiled, and began to tell me how much she hates her job, and how I was lucky to have a job that I loved. I agreed and realized how truly thankful I was. My job and my life were just perfect for me.

The plane landed, and I wished her well. She asked where I was flying to on my next flight.

'Off to Paris, then Israel for the weekend," I said with a glimmer of excitement.

She sighed. All I could think about was when we were growing up how she and her dad would say all the time how she was going to be the best attorney ever. She would study all the time and take as many honor courses as possible, working toward that dream. She achieved her dream.

I snickered as I remembered that she would tell me and everyone else who did not take AP classes that we were not 'going places', that she was the smartest of the group, and knew exactly what she was going to do in life. Like many of us graduating high school, we had ideas of what path we should take, maybe not as clear as hers, but like most I was told I would figure it out at the right time, and seeing her at the airport, reminded me, I had.

While I had found my niche, there was turbulence brewing in my industry. In 1990, my life had taken an unexpected turn. The airline industry was changing rapidly and Pan Am was sinking fast. The outlook was not good for my career. Our union told us that United would only take the first 2,000.

At the time I was number 4,500. You can do the math. Needless to say, I was in debt up to my eyeballs, and I could not get any help from family or friends. This sudden change was impacting me hard.

I was dating a man who was gorgeous, had a great job, and allowed me to 'check all the boxes.'

I thought, maybe he could be the one. It turns out things are not always as they seem. Not only was the man not interested in marriage, but he was already married, and had been divorced two other times prior. He was also dating another woman while dating me - from the same airline. My husband meter might have been skewed. He was not the great catch I thought.

Realizing I needed to make quick changes to survive, I quickly put out resumes to all the airlines and was asked by Delta and American to come for an interview. I accepted the interview with Delta first because they were the highest paying airline, and also had a base in Miami.

I was hired on-the-spot and began training that week. My financial situation was very bleak and in the red, but with this opportunity, things were at least starting to look up.

I got a roommate who worked for Pan Am as a gate agent, and that quickly helped pay half the rent in my Miami house. After completing training for Delta, I was based in Orlando. Delta did not allow commuting for the first six months of my career, which presented another logistical nightmare and more financial hardship in gas money, and impact on my time for travel and logistics.

At the time, I was paying for a mortgage on a house that I did not even get to enjoy. I was paying for a rental apartment, including rental furniture and a car payment. Just when I thought things couldn't get any worse, Delta decided to merge with Pan Am. I lost all of my seniority, not to mention they did not take everyone from the company, and this made a very uncomfortable time at work. I knew some of my friends had jobs, while others did not. I was afraid to contact anyone, not sure if they had a job, or worse, that they might hit me up for money. Life was stressful and bleak at this time. I had to put my house in Miami up for sale and start recovering.

Have you ever watched the show Mary Tyler Moore, where she throws her hat up in the air and the song lyrics are playing, "you're going to make it after all?" That was how I felt just a few months prior. But, at this moment, just a few months later, I felt like I was drowning, and there was no escape or help coming.

To add to the somber mood of the day, a good friend from Pan Am called to say his cousin Enrique, who was also a flight attendant with Pan Am, had Aids. Enrique and I were the same size, and we had a great- time together shopping all over the world, trying on each other's outfits, and laughing constantly through our travel adventures. Enrique passed away within a few months. Just two days prior, I had lost another friend to Aids. I was at my breaking point emotionally, physically, and spiritually. It seemed I could not catch a break, and I felt like I was being swallowed up. I did everything I knew to do according to my religion and upbringing. I prayed and fasted, yet nothing was giving me relief. I just kept moving through the moments, hoping something would turn around.

Then in February of 1992, my life changed forever. Like most new hires, I was on call. I remember it was late in the evening and knew that there were only a few flights left - a flight to Germany and a flight to Las Vegas, neither appealed to me, but I could use the money. I called scheduling to see how far I was on the list. I was told I would be used, and to be ready to go. I got everything ready and put my uniform on. That's when the weather got bad, and the phone rang with scheduling telling me that they were extending my call window until 2:00 am. I took off my shoes, put a pot of coffee on, and turned the on TV.

I started channel surfing and came upon this channel called the 700 Club. The people were talking about these deep, personal issues. One woman had an abortion, and another man attempted to kill himself by blowing off his head, and I was amazed the man looked like someone had shrunk his head like in the movie Beetlejuice. I was awed by what I was seeing. Their stories captivated me. For some odd reason, I sat glued to the TV, engaged in the entire program.

I was hearing their pain and, how they all said that in spite of it, they have joy. I wondered how this could be possible. Then a man named Dr. Roberts began to speak. I thought to myself *a Doctor, finally someone who knows how to fix this mess I am in*. I sat up, turned the volume up, and listened more intently.

Finally, I will hear an answer and find what I have been looking for - how to make things better. Well, no sooner did my joy turn into sorrow when he said, "Jesus Christ is the answer." I got so mad and was furious at myself, *how could I have fallen for this?*

I began to look for the remote, found it, and picked it up.

But, right then, Pat Roberts said, "YOUNG LADY, PUT DOWN THAT REMOTE - GOD IS TALKING TO YOU."

I threw the remote down with such fear as I looked around the room to see if Pat Roberts was behind me, or worse - God. I was shaking, as Dr. Robert's began to say, "God hears you and wants to heal you in every place you hurt, and the only way to do that, is to accept Jesus Christ into your life."

At this point I started talking to the TV, "what do I do?"

Pat Roberts kept speaking, as if directly to me.

"It's simple," he said. "Just put your hands on the TV, and repeat after me, and I am telling you, you will hear from God Almighty."

In my mind I was wondering *is this what Ms. Dodie meant?*

All of a sudden, I had this deep desire to hear from God. I wanted to know! Was this the missing link in my life? Will this complete me and make me happy, and take away all my pain and sorrow? Will this .... The feeling of urgency and concern came upon me all at once as my mind raced with questions and I was overcome.

I put my hand on the TV, and as soon as I did, I could hear my deceased grandmother's voice telling me in her thick accent, "What are you kidding me? I always talked to you this way. "

I remember saying to God, "Please forgive me if this is not from you. Kill me now if this is wrong."

I said the prayer, and absolutely nothing happened. Nothing!

Zip, nada, nothing!

You see, Lillian, my crazy Evangelical girlfriend, had explained that when you accept Christ in your life, your life would change, and I would become part of a king's dynasty.

As you can imagine, I was thinking robes, crowns and definitely a red carpet. I would be like Miss America, or the Queen of England. I looked around and noticed the time, it was almost 1:00 a.m., and I saw no crown, and no red carpet.

Disappointed, I called scheduling to see what my status was, to which the scheduler replied, "You are released from your window, and you have a trip scheduled for tomorrow at 8:00 a. m."

"Great," I said, deflated from what seemed like yet another disappointment.

I hung up the phone and thought to myself that I had truly lost my mind. I went to my bedroom and started getting ready for bed. I set my alarm and hung up my uniform. I turned the lights off and was about to crawl into the bed.

But, that is when I noticed there was this bright light on the ceiling over my bed. I did not expect that, and I was suddenly alert again. I thought to myself, *not again.*

You see, I live on the top floor of an apartment complex and two weeks prior we had horrible rain and hail storms that caused a leak in the ceiling to which the lights from outside shone through. I stood on top of the bed to see if I had a leak again. I pushed my fingers to see where the leak was. I nearly cracked my fingers on the popcorn ceiling as it did not yield to my poking around.

Thank goodness, no leak, I thought to myself. I turned my head to the curtains, thinking it must be the street light reflecting. I jumped off the bed and went to the curtains to readjust them, and that is when I noticed the light getting brighter. There was no reasonable source, and no one else in the room; the television was off, and so were the lights, and here I was in a dark apartment bedroom, with this light growing brighter and brighter.

Earlier that week I was watching TV about alien abductions and thought maybe that's what was happening, as there was absolutely no other explanation. I jumped into the bed, pulled the cover over my eyes and asked God to, "please save me!"

Hearing me speak, I got hold of myself and realized this was it, God is going to kill me, and I had offended God by all that television babble.

But, that is when another light appeared and got bigger and stronger, and brighter. Soon the light had completely engulfed me. I don't know how else to explain it, but, I felt peace, there was no fear, and nothing remotely related to my idea of aliens. Then something even more miraculous happened, and I had this feeling of warmth cover my entire body. I felt the heat from my insides to my outsides; there was not one place I did not feel the presence of this heat.

You see a few years ago I was in a bad accident, which had long-term effects; one of the effects was on my knee. My knee would swell to the size of a softball and I would have to get it drained followed by physical therapy and cortisone injections to ease the pain. I just had my knee drained about a week ago and the pain was intense. At that moment when the lights hit me I literally felt no pain. I felt like liquid love being poured all over me. Than just as fast as it appeared it disappeared.

> "For with you is the fountain of life; In Your light we see light."
>
> Psalm 36:9

> "When Jesus spoke again to the people, he said, "I am the light of the world. Whoever follows me will never walk in darkness but will have the light of life."
>
> John 8:12

I fell fast asleep and woke up so refreshed - it truly was the best night sleep I ever had. I went to work and thought *do I tell anyone?*

I was not sure what happened. So, I thought I best keep it to myself, just in case someone thinks I am crazy, and certainly not to my family, they would disown me right there.

Chapter Six

THE SILENT YEARS

M̲y alarm clock sounds off at 6:00 AM. I shot out of bed, looking to see if the light was still there. I noticed everything looked the same, minus the light. I started to doubt if I had actually encountered the light.

I began my routine of getting ready and packing up everything I will need for my trip. As I started to turn off all the lights and leave my bedroom I heard this voice that made me stop dead in my tracks. I hear the voice say BELIEVE.

I pick up my suitcase that I had just dropped on the floor, in shock, and promptly walked out of my apartment shaking. I could barely manage to put the key in the door to lock it behind me. I get in my car for the twenty-minute drive to the airport. A part of me was illuminated that I just had an encounter with God, and another part of me was simultaneously overwhelmed and terrified.

I reached the employee parking lot and found a space right away - that was a miracle in itself. Usually, that early in the morning, everyone is fighting for a parking space so they will not have to go to the overflow lot. As I sat in my car for a minute trying to wrap my mind on what happened last night, I see the shuttle bus turning the corner. I quickly jump out of my car, grab my bag, and run for the bus. The driver of the bus opens the door and greets me with a warm smile. I really needed that, and I smile back.

We arrive at the crew sign-in area, and I am the only one left on the bus. I tell the driver 'thank you' and he says to me, "Have a Blessed day," and smiles back. I look at him and wonder if he knows what just happened to me? Getting off the bus, I see a friend of mine. My friend and I went through in- flight training together for Delta, her name is Sheri. Her dad is a minister. Sheri is one of those girls who is always smiling and never says anything bad about anyone, or any situation, regardless of the circumstances. She also never shoved her religion down on me.

While I was getting off the bus she was getting on.

"Have a great trip," she said with a great, big smile.

I told her to enjoy her time off. She stopped mid-step and turns to me to ask, "Did you do something different?"

Shocked, I shake my head side to side, to demonstrate an emphatic "No!" and ran off the bus. I was confused as to what just happened, and filled with more questions than with answers.

I made my sign-in and met the crew on board the airplane for our departing flight. I was the last to get there, which meant I worked first class. It was a simple turnaround from Orlando to New York. This was going to be quick and easy, so I thought.

While working first class, a man entered the aircraft. He looked Middle Eastern and had this big smile on his face and one of those religious collars on his starched top. He placed his items in the overhead in first class. I went up to him with a warm smile and asked if I could take his coat, and offered him something to drink. He smiled back, looked me straight into my eyes and said, "I can see the glory of God upon you."

I smiled back, not sure what to do; on the inside I am freaking out. In my mind, I am asking myself how he knows.

I go to the back of the airplane, looking for the flight attendant with a cross on. I run up to her and ask, "Do you see anything on me?"

"Turn around," she motioned with her hand as she looked intently to spot-check my uniform.

"I do." then she says, "Smile."

I do, and she says "I can't see anything." I go back to first class and continue my duties. The Flight Attendant in charge asks if everything is alright. I said, "Yes, just a strange conversation with the man in sitting in 3A."

The Flight attendant looks to see who is sitting in the seat and says, "Do you know who that is?"

I shake my head to indicate no, as she says, "That is Pastor Benny Hinn. He's on all the posters when you first come in, and when you go out of the airport."

I shake my head implying 'yea, that is where I have seen him.'

The Flight attendant says, "He is world famous. I wonder why he doesn't have his own jet."

This encounter left me perplexed and shaken the rest of the trip.

A couple of weeks had passed from the time with my unexpected encounter with Pastor Benny Hinn. I had recently taken in a commuter to board with me and help supplement my income. She was also a flight attendant with Delta who went to initial training with me and had been with another airline as well. She and I were home at the same time, which rarely every happened. I heard my doorbell ring. I was in the back bedroom doing some paperwork and knew it would take me a minute to get to the door.

I shouted for the roommate to get the door, but then I heard the shower water running. I quickly ran to the door, aware of the obvious delay now. I looked through the peephole and saw no one there. Hesitantly, I opened the door, looking side to side to see who it was and still saw no one. I looked down, hoping to see a package from UPS; we were both expecting our new uniform pieces, and they were expected to arrive sometime that week.

When I opened the door, there were no boxes, but a black bible lay on the floor. I picked up the bible and put it on the kitchen counter; perplexed who would have left it. When my commuter got out of the shower, I asked if she ordered a bible. She smiled and immediately scoffs, "Me? No, way."

She assures me that it's probably from the Mormons or Jehovah witnesses, and in the same breath encourages me to "just throw it out."

"Throw it out?" I am shocked. "That is sacrilegious."

I explain to her that it has the name of God in it, and you can't do that. To which she replied not phased in the least, "Whatever."

I could not throw out the bible, regardless who sent it. I kept that bible and told her I was afraid if I throw the bible out something bad would happen to us.

Several months later, I was on call again, this time it was to a destination I liked. I was flying to Los Angeles, relieved it was a non-stop trip. When I arrived on board the aircraft, it was apparent I was the only flight attendant based in Orlando, and everyone else was based out of Portland.

I found out I was replacing a flight attendant who got sick at the last minute. The crew I was working with just did an all-nighter (a trip that starts at any time after 8:00

PM and arrives any time before 8:00 AM) and they were doing the last leg of their trip. This means they were all tired and ready to be home. Unfortunately, I would be going to the hotel by myself.

The flight was full, and everyone on the crew was exhausted. As we finished the meal service, the galley flight attendant began to cry to the other flight attendant working the back of the airplane, who was also the lead flight attendant. I had nowhere to go, the plane was completely full, and I was forced into this intimate exchange.

The flight attendant crying was Asian, and was telling the other flight attendant how her sister and brother-in-law just became Christians. I stopped dead in my tracks. I could not move my feet, it was if they were glued to the floor. I knew it was not polite to eaves drop in such a personal conversation but, I could not help myself.

I continued to listen to what they were talking about. I started to clean up the galley and do busy work to make it appear I was not listening to their conversation. The other flight attendant was very sympathetic and kept telling her how sorry she was. I don't know what overcame me but, I jumped in on their conversation and asked, "why is being a Christian such a bad thing?"

The other flight attendant listening to the Asian flight attendant quickly excused herself, "I need to start the movie."

The Asian flight attendant said "My family and I worship Buddha! My father is a man of importance in our temple."

"That must have been hard for your sister to tell everyone," I offered.

The flight attendant shared softly that her parents have disowned her sister.

"That has to be hard for you," I said. And, she agreed, dropping her face down with sadness.

Then I muster my courage to share my experience. "I don't think this is a coincidence that I am on this flight."

She perked up, but remained unsure of what I meant.

I don't know why I said what I said but, I began to share my story about what just happened to me - lights and all. The flight attendant was very impressed.

"WOW, that is exactly what happened with my brother -in- law," she exclaimed.

I asked her what she meant; thinking maybe she could explain to me and help me understand what the heck was going on.

She explained that her brother-in-law had been under tremendous pressure from work and was told he would be relocating to China, and that her sister did not want to leave her family and friends. She went on to say that her brother-in-law was contemplating suicide because he did not want to divorce his wife, and he hated his job. Her brother-in-law went to a co-worker and told him what was going on, and the man told him about Jesus. Her brother-in-law accepted Jesus, and the same light you saw, he saw.

When my brother-in-law started changing, my sister began to question her husband. Her husband confided to my sister, and that is when he told her what happened to him. At first, my sister doubted what he told her but, then, she started noticing little changes. Her husband was hardly ever angry, anymore, and always had a smile on his face. My brother-in-law always had a bible in his hand, and would be reading it all thorough out the day. Soon, my sister became envious of her husband, because of the joy he had, and how it seemed nothing bothered him. My brother-in- law convinced my sister to become a Christian, too.

"Wow!" I was excited to hear such a transformation, "What happened to them?" She said her brother-in-law works for some Christian organization, along with her sister, and they were moving away to become missionaries.

I asked her if her sister and brother-in-law were happy, and she smiled and said, "I have never seen them happier."

"Don't you find this strange that your brother-in-law and sister accepted Christ, and now here I am?" I asked her. "I think God is also talking to you."

"I don't know what to think, perhaps you are right," she agreed.

"It's just like me with the remote." I assured her.

She looked panicked and I said, "We all have this same peace, don't you want that? It sure beats crying over things."

She tells me she does not want to be disowned by her family, like her sister, because she is not married.

"I'm not married," I say matter-of-factly. I didn't share with her that I had not yet told my family, which would probably have me disowned, too.

She smiled and said, "Perhaps you are right, what did you do?"

I told her how I put my hands on the TV. She said to me, with a huff, "There are no TV's on the aircraft, besides my brother-in-law and sister just said something."

"Do you remember what you said?" I shake my head no "but, I do remember saying Jesus. "

"That's it?" she asks, unsure.

I shake my head yes.

Just then, the flight attendant comes over the PA and announces the movie will start momentarily, which is our cue to begin our drink service. We both leave the galley and begin our work. At this point of the flight, we each get a rest break. Unfortunately, we had different rest break schedules and were unable to continue the conversation.

As the plane touched down and everyone was getting off the plane, the pilot assigned me to me contact crew operations. I rushed to the phone on the jet way and called crew ops. I was told that I had a schedule change to my rotation. My departure time for tomorrow was to be pushed up earlier by four hours, and the hotel would not be in the downtown area. Additionally, I needed to pick up a voucher at the flight attendant lounge.

I headed back into the aircraft to gather all my belonging and hoping to run into the Asian flight attendant to finish our conversation. As I was packing up all my personal belongings, a supervisor came on board the aircraft and asked if I was the Orlando- based flight attendant. I confirmed I was. She then handed me the voucher to the hotel and encouraged me to hurry so that I could catch the shuttle, leaving in just ten minutes. I had missed the opportunity with the attendant.

Just a little history reminder, The L.A. riots began in April of 1992, plus the terminal was getting a face lift which meant it was a hike through the terminal, due to construction. I got to the baggage claim, picked up the shuttle bus, and went to the hotel. It was early afternoon and I had not eaten all day; I was hungry. There was nothing around the hotel, not even a coffee shop. I inquired of the hotel receptionist if there was a nearby mall, thinking I could pick something up to eat from the food court.

The gentleman directs me to a mall close by, but I should think about taking a taxi.

"No thanks," I reply, as I head out the revolving doors. "I could use the fresh air."

Within twenty minutes, I'm at the mall. I shop around for a few minutes, and ask a clerk, "where is the food court?"

"Sorry the food court is closed due to construction, but there are several nice restaurants just a few blocks down the road," he offers.

"Are they in walking distance?" I ask, "I don't have a car."

"Yes, just be careful," he said, "and, look for the fork in the road."

I never found the fork in the road, even after walking for several minutes. At this point, my stomach is talking to me, and I look up to see the golden arches of McDonalds. I pick up my pace and head inside. As soon as I entered, I noticed everyone was looking at me. I naturally looked down at myself making sure everything is zipped and in place.

As I looked up, that is when I noticed that I was the only white person around and that many of the African Americans had similar tattoos on their necks. I knew these were signs of a gang membership. I thought to myself, *if I leave, I could be hurt, if I stay I am better off.* I shake off my fear and head to the counter.

I order my food and scan the room for a place to sit. That is when I notice the kid's area and walked that way. Thankfully, there was an empty table, and I sat down. That is when I noticed all the kids had on the same yellow t-shirt.

The man sitting next to me with the same yellow t-shirt says, "Are you lost?"

We both started laughing. "Come over here," the man said to me, and I moved closer.

"What are you doing here?" he asked. I told him "I am a flight attendant on a layover." I asked him about the t-shirts, he said that "these are the kids from my church and they just came back from a retreat." He reached out his hand and said, I'm Pastor EV Hill." I shook his hand and told him my name.

I told him that I used to be a youth advisor for my synagogue. He asked me, "Are you a Christian?" Not sure how to respond, I figured he was a pastor, he should know things, so I began to tell him everything that happened and then I told him how stranger things have been happening to me.

"Like what?" he asked.

The thing with Pastor Benny Hinn, and then I shared with him how a bible showed up on my doorstep one day, and when I told him that a flight attendant told me to throw it out because it's probably from one of those Jehovah witnesses or Mormons and was told that their bible is different than ours, leaving me confused. I kept the bible mostly because it had the name of God and knew better than to throw out anything with God's name on it.

The pastor kept saying, "Hmm." Then he encouraged me, by saying "you need to start reading the New Testament."

My jaw dropped, how did he know that I would only read the Old Testament? He smiled and asked, "Is that all?" I shook my head no and began to tell him my fears and how strange things kept happening, even beyond that, citing my encounter with the Asian attendant.

The Pastor smiled and said, "This is what you need to do." This made me sit up in the chair and listen more intently. The pastor said, "Next time you hear something go bump in the night, or a fear comes on you, you say the following, "Satan is that all you got?"

"What?" I exclaimed, "Are you crazy? Why would I want to say that?"

"Let me finish," he said, as he stands up, puts his hands on his hips, and says "Jesus - then you say JESUS! And move to the side. And, say, "Jesus, it's all yours."

I smiled and so did the pastor.

"It's almost dark. This young man will walk you back to the mall," he said motioning to a volunteer, sitting in the next booth.

"Thank you and it was a pleasure to meet you," I said.

"Likewise" he said, and shook my hand, as we parted.

As I left the McDonald's and started walking, I could not help but ask the young man "is it really that bad for me to be here?" The young man started laughing and said "Yes, the only white woman I see around here are drug dealers and hookers."

As we started to walk back, the young man said, "Come on, we need to cut through this field." I resisted as I said, "I walked on a road the entire time."

"That is impossible!" he said, as he looked oddly at me. "There has never been a road here." As we came to the end of the field, there was the street with all the restaurants and mall before us.

I thanked the young man, and offered him some money."

"Na, I don't think I am supposed to, but I am sure going to remember this night!" we both smiled and nodded, and walked our different paths.

> "In all your ways acknowledge him, and he
> will make straight your paths."
> -Proverbs 3:6

I walked back to the hotel and the receptionist greeted me with relief, "I was getting worried about you and was just about to call my manager."

I thanked him for thinking of me, but asked, "Why?" He said the riots are still going on and we are telling the guests to not go out after dark, and always walk with someone. "Thank you God," I uttered, to which he said, "Amen."

As I started to get ready for bed and put everything into my suitcase, a feeling of uneasiness came over me, no doubt from the comforting words of the receptionist, but, then the bathroom lights began to flicker. I went into the bathroom and flipped the switch a hundred times and still it would not shut off. I closed the door and could see the lights going on and off; I took the comforter off the bed and placed it by the door to shut out the psychedelic flashing of the light.

At this point, I couldn't sleep, no matter how much I told myself to forget about it. I called down to the operator, asking if there were any maintenance men who could fix the light in the bathroom. I was told someone would be up there in a few minutes. I quickly got dressed and heard a knock at the door. I thought *wow that was fast*.

I moved the comforter from the floor onto the chair, and greeted the maintenance man, who asked which light to check. I point to the bathroom, and when he flips the switch, it goes off normally.

Now, I'm mad, I tell him that I did that, and it did not work. He just smiled at me and left. I lock up, and change clothes for the night. I don't touch the bathroom light, and quickly jump into bed. Bam! The light starts flickering. I know better than to call again for assistance. I put the comforter back on the floor but through the edges of the door frame, I can see the light continuing to go off and on.

At this point, I could not sleep and crippling fear over took me. I got out of bed, put my hand on my hips and with fear and trembling said, "Satan is that all you got?" Just then, the phone rings. I won't begin to tell you what I was thinking. I pick up the phone, and no one was there. I could feel the beads of perspiration on my lip, and my hair was sticking to my neck, at this point.

I was petrified, and then I said, "OK, Jesus come on NOW!"

The lights stopped flickering and this feeling of peace came over me. That night I slept hard and never woke till my alarm went off.

As I look back on all these encounters, I realized, the enemy was trying to instill fear in me and have me deny my new faith, but God was seeking me and pursing me, and an ever present help, even then. That pastor from the McDonald's was right about that!

I did not ask for this journey yet, through God's infinite wisdom, He put all these people in my path, so I would find my way to Truth and to Him. Perhaps, you are reading this book because someone suggested this to you or you accidently purchased this book. There are no accidents, or coincidences in the Kingdom of God; they are all appointments designed by God.

> [11] For I know the plans I have for you," declares the LORD, "plans to prosper you and not to harm you, plans to give you hope and a future. [12] Then you will call on me and come and pray to me, and I will listen to you. [13] You will seek me and find me when you seek me with all your heart.
>
> Jeremiah 29:11-12

On a side note, I never realized who EV Hill was until after I married and had moved to Atlanta and saw him on the TV. I could not believe my eyes, I was cleaning my house and had turned on the TBN channel, and there was the man with the yellow t-shirt from McDonald's. Mr. Crouch was introducing Pastor EV Hill as the leading pastor of some super church in L.A. Pastor Hill, explained how he helped with bringing peace to L.A. during the riots, and how he assisted people all over the world. My jaw dropped. I thanked God for allowing me to meet such an important man of God.

Chapter Seven

HEADS IN THE CLOUD

In 1992, on one particular day, I received a call from my mom.

"The strangest thing has happened," my mom said.

"What?" I asked, perplexed at her opening statement.

She began to tell me that she received a letter, but it was not addressed to her; it was addressed to me.

"Is it a postcard that I sent you?" I asked, thinking through my recent travel destinations, and wondering if I had mailed her a postcard, without remembering.

"No," there is a letter addressed to you, but, oddly, it's from you," she said.

Mom asked if she could open it. She couldn't understand what was in this letter. "Yes, of course, I'm curious to know what's in it!"I said, not remembering a time I mailed myself a letter.

My mom started reading the letter to aloud to herself, and stopped mid-way, "Oh, Cin, you need to read this on your own."

I was laughing awkwardly, not remembering the letter, at first.

"What? Are you kidding me?" I wanted to know what the letter said right then. "You can't do that to me. What's in the letter, already?"

"Well, it's a letter addressed to you, from you." That's odd; I don't remember writing a letter to myself.

"The strangest part of this letter is that it is dated from ten years ago!" she said.

"Mom, this is crazy, what's in the letter?" I was getting anxious to know the content of the letter to myself.

Mom read the letter to me, and as she read the letter, it came to me the time I penned this letter. In high school, my home economics teacher said that she was going to mail letters that we wrote to ourselves to remind us of who we are and where we wanted to be in life. My mom and I had a good laugh but, it gave me such a deeper desire to get back on track to some of my life goals.

After reading the letter, it occurred to me that I have accomplished almost all of the goals I had set for myself, such as flying all over the world, to swim in all the oceans of the world, learn a new language, and then there were those I'm sure would be yet to come: live on a farm with horses and llamas, and, to be married with five or six kids.

My mom commented on how fortunate I was to be able to have accomplished so much already. Indeed, I was, yet, the desire for a family came upon me. I no longer looked at men quite the same, weighing the possibility of matrimony. I must admit, I never had thoughts and dreams about my wedding like most girls, no doubt because of all the crazy couples I met and lived near, and, not to mention family members.

Yes, marriage was never a high priority for me but, like most women of that time when their parents would complain about not being married, I would find a nice guy to bring home, and this usually did the trick. I am embarrassed to admit that I have been engaged several times, especially when Oprah came out with that lovely show explaining women over the age of thirty not married were more likely to be killed by a terrorist than to get married - truthfully, in my line of work, probably truer than fiction, because of the demands of my career.

My grandpa would always say "What's the rush?" So, I never pursued it.

As life would have it, in 1994, I married a friend who I had known for years. We both were working for Delta. I was a flight attendant, he was a pilot. We were living in Orlando and my husband was commuting from Orlando to New York. Life was wonderful. I will also tell you, I was still a closet Christian, only my friend Lillian knew, Pastor Benny Hinn, and EV Hill - not bad for a short- list.

Being over a certain age I realized I needed to get on the baby wagon if I was going to have a child. My mom would remind me of all her difficulties conceiving, and encouraging me to get busy. After two years of wedding bliss, my husband tells me the airplane he is on is becoming very senior and he will be on call all the time. For those of you not familiar with these terms, it basically means he's at the beck and call of the airline. In other words, commuting is out of the question. With a heavy heart I put in my transfer and went to New York with him.

We packed up the U-Haul and headed for Long Island, I can still hear my sister say to me, this is crazy the only thing on Long Island is Joey Buttafuoco and the Long Island Lolita. Wow, she is right, I don't know anyone there. Thank goodness I had family in other parts of New York. At this point, I was still 'in the closet' as a Christian and keeping that door shut, until I could sort things out and figure out what was really going on.

We settled into our new house which my husband had purchased many years ago when he was working for Pan Am. I might add he never updated the house, it was always used as a crash pad, and it reflected this when we moved there (*yuck, is all I can say*).

Things had vastly changed in the flight attendant lounge when I worked for Pan Am, based in New York. I was now working for Delta as a flight attendant. I was required to be available for all three airports; Kennedy, LaGuardia and Newark.

Like most New Yorkers, we had one car. In case you were wondering, let me share with you my first experience driving in New York. It was simple, I was going from Kennedy airport to LaGuardia; an easy trip, one highway - easy peasy.

The driver in front of me is in a minivan; I am feeling great, because I can see through the van that the woman driver has kids in car seats. I think this is a good person to be behind (safe and slow).

New York drivers they are very creative in their thinking, and, as a driver, you have to be ready for anything. All of a sudden, the woman who is driving the minivan is now driving on the median. I slow down when the car behind me honks and goes around me and is also driving on the medium. Unlike most people, who live anywhere other than New York, when you see a tire rolling by, you stop and offer assistance to the person whose tire is rolling down the highway. This was not the case, everyone slowed down enough to look and to continue on either of the medians, or intersecting the other lane. So, I stopped my car and put my hazard lights on, giving the man time to get his tire. The man looks up and asks, "Are you going to rob me?"

Life lesson learned, follow the flow of traffic, while driving in New York.

We lived on Long Island, close to Hofstra University. Going to Kennedy Airport was just a thirty -minute ride, and LaGuardia was little over forty minutes. The problem was Newark airport; it's a schlep (far distance and a hassle). In order for me to fly out of Newark, I needed to take the Verrazano Bridge. If you have never seen the Verrazano bridge google it, it is a sight to behold. As I mentioned before, I lived in Florida, the flat lands. The only bridge is in 'little Haiti' where ships pass under, in other words they may have been long, but definitely not tall. This was not the case of the Verrazano Bridge; it is some bridge to drive.

You can imagine driving in New York is a thrill in itself, but adds the busiest bridge, not to mention the tallest bridge. It is rush hour traffic, and like most normal drivers, you stay in the right lane. Because the right lane goes slower, and people won't honk as much, you stay in the right lane. The bridge started going up, *as I was driving*. Let me rephrase that, I was driving and the bridge went *completely vertical*.

The problem was that I chose the right lane, which meant that my lane and the one next to me also went high, high up. I did not know this until my car was continuously shifting and I could feel my body leaning further back. I turned my head to the right. Big Mistake!!! I saw all the way down. The water was massive, but the ships looked like bath toys, and I thought I just took off the runway soaring through the clouds. I began to feel the bridge sway. Panic crippled me and I peed in my pants and could not move.

Everyone is honking at me and giving me the dirtiest looks as they would pass by. I did not care I was not moving. After about fifteen minutes this policeman came up and tapped on my window asked what was wrong.

I begin to cry and say, "Who in their right minds builds an amusement adventure on a highway?" The policeman asks, "Can you move your car?"

I just shook my head, scared that if I moved, I will fall off the bridge. The policeman screamed in his walkie-talkie, "It's not a jumper."

I look up and he says to me, "Move Over."

I respond in terror, "I can't."

The policeman in his most calming New York accent voice says, "Lady you have a conga line going on, and people are getting upset because they are going to be late for work!"

Not only do I feel bad, but, now comes the ultimate of humiliation, I wanted to lie and say I spilled my coffee but, I didn't even have a cup to prove it. I just blurted out I peed in my pants. The policeman looks displeased and asks me if I have anything he could sit on. I shake my head, he then opens the door behind me reached for the car mat, slams the door, and tells me to slide over. I slide over, with tears running down my face; he throws the mat on the front seat and sits on it, in order to move my car, and, get the conga line going.

He sees, I am wearing my flight uniform and says, "You a stewardess?" It wasn't a question more of a statement and then he says, "Don't you guys fly over 10,000 feet?" "Yes, I said, but we are in an airplane that has wings and pilot who is licensed to fly!" He starts laughing and tells me, "I picked the wrong profession to be afraid of heights."

At this point I could care less what he is saying or thinking, we just reached the point of the arch, I saw clouds and no birds were near. We finally get to the end of the bridge and the policeman proceeds to tell me another way to travel so I will not cause an accident or kill anyone. I tell him Thank You and I assured him I will NEVER take this bridge as long as I live!

After that point, I only took trips out of Kennedy and LaGuardia. The problem was when my husband or I went to Kennedy, while the other was going to LaGuardia. We decided that the person who goes to LaGuardia would get the car and the person who goes out of Kennedy would take the bus – it worked.

Because we lived near Hofstra University there were several hotel chains that offered courtesy shuttles from the airport to the hotel. It saved us a tremendous amount of money and, we were happy to tip the drivers.

One such time, I had to take the shuttle. It was raining hard and it was late at night. The van was filled with a bunch of pilots and several business men, all in suits. I waited to see if there was room to jump in. The driver knew me and said, "Come on in."

I got into the front row when a man quickly jumps in next to me. I was in the middle seat. The rain started coming down real hard. You can tell people were concerned because everyone's conversation stopped, and all were looking outside.

There was this voice I heard in my head that said, "Put your seatbelt on." At first, I dismissed it and thought, *no, we are almost there.* I heard the voice again say, "Put your seatbelt on." I thought *is that God talking to me?* I turned around to grab my seat belt, but it was broken. Instead, I grabbed it, as an anchor. The van crashed into the car in front of us as the driver slammed on his brakes, in the middle of the highway.

My face slammed into the driver's seat while my arm got a burn from the seatbelt wrapped around it, preventing me from going through the front windshield. Everyone in the van sees me flying, and relieved nothing more than a chipped tooth.

As we arrived at the hotel, my husband was there to pick me up. He sees blood on my face and I quickly tell him what happened. I tell him that this man slammed on his brakes in the middle of the highway and we crashed into them. I took a face plant into the driver's seat. My husband asked,"Why didn't you have your seatbelt fastened?"

Irritated, I explained in a displeasing voice, "I would if I could have, but, the seat belt was broken." My husband realized the severity of what could have happened, and agreed, "Someone was certainly looking out for you."

I had forgotten all about that time when I had an infamous conversation with him. It seemed he had been listening.

Chapter Eight

WE NEED THE ROOM–
IT IS REAL!!

On one of my flights, I met a flight attendant who was a heavy smoker, and had a very loud (potty mouth). Here we are working on a small airplane, and there is nowhere to hide. The load was light, yet we kept bumping into each other and both tried to be civilized with the other. The plane landed and we head to our lay-over hotel.

Thank goodness the hotel is close to the airport, and even better, the next day we only have one leg to work together and we are all finished for the day.

As we head off the shuttle to the hotel, the loud flight attendant offers to me and another flight attendant "lets meet in twenty minutes and we all can grab dinner?" "Great," we both replied. We all head to our rooms. I quickly change and head downstairs. As I am walking in the lobby I can see the flight attendant who is very loud, but not the other flight attendant. "Look, I know you are a smoker and I don't like to eat where there is smoke."

"Me either," she agreed and grabbed my elbow, steering us to the dining room.

I was already anticipating the discomfort of dinner and thinking to myself to order soup and salad, which will be the quickest thing I can get and be finished fast.

As we are seated and the hostess hands us our menu, I scan it over and realize I'm starving, and a soup and salad just won't do. The waitress has already approached our table to ask, "What would you like to drink?"

"Water for me," I say, followed closely by the other flight attendant.

"I'll have some wine, want to split a bottle?"she asked.

"No, thanks," I said.

"Ok," then, I'll have half a carafe."

I'm thinking *lush and smoker what a lovely combination, please God bring the food now* but, we had not yet even ordered.

Just then, she slams down her first glass of wine.

"Are you a Christian?" She asked me.

I nearly spit the water out of my mouth; I was clearly not expecting that.

"Excuse me?" I managed to get out calmly.

She asked again, "Are you a Christian?"

I looked puzzled and thought, *is she trying to be antagonistic?* I could not speak.

She began to tell me that she just met this flight attendant on her flight that was handsome, but 'religious'. I just kept listening and nodding. She continued to share and said that this flight attendant started talking to her about Jesus, and that she was raised Catholic and never knew about Jesus the way this flight attendant explained it.

"What do you mean?" I asked.

Apparently, this flight attendant made Jesus not only to be God, but a friend. *Interesting,* I thought to myself.

"Do you believe in Jesus?"She asked again with persistence

I just wanted this evening to end, but something inside of me just blurted out my story - lights and all. I could not believe I just laid it all on the table. Her jaw dropped, and at this point, the carafe was empty. Again, she asked if I wanted some wine, too.

"No thanks," I said, and added, "to be honest, I'm trying to get pregnant."

She smiled and said she was trying to figure things out herself.

She shared how she had found a radio station that only played Christian music and that they feature people who explain things about the Bible. She was very excited about this radio station, and continued to gush about how she listened all the time, especially, to this woman named Joyce Meyers.

"She sounds Jewish," I said, then I asked her, "is she Jewish?"

"I don't know," she answered with a puzzled face.

We finished our meals and she jotted her phone number on a small piece of paper, along with the radio station setting, and invited me to, "keep in touch."

"Okay, sounds good," I agreed, and for some strange reason, I actually believed I would.

Weeks passed and we made contact with each other, eventually we agree to get together for lunch and shopping. Our friendship grew and we met up at least once a month and shared our stories of work and what we were learning from the bible. It's a friendship that started blossoming.

I share with her that on one of my trips, I had met a flight attendant who was also trying to get pregnant and she had shared with me the name and number of the doctor she was using for infertility.

On a side note, for those not familiar, flight attendants who share a jump seat, are also known as shrink seats. The jump seat is where you can find a plethora of information on any subject.

I quickly call the infertility specialist and make an appointment. My husband encourages me to, "check it out and let me know."

I had to wait two months and went to meet the doctor, a short, Asian woman. She was quick to say that we would first need to do some tests to dismiss any problems with either spouse, (let the cash register ring).

I tell her that we had conceived one time but, I did not know I was pregnant; I lost the baby within weeks. She told me that I needed to stop flying and find another job that does not involve going up in the air. I applied for a ground job that evening and was hired within a week as an Operational Supervisor. I loved my boss, but the hours were not that great, and I soon changed from Operational Supervisor to Human Resource Source Supervisor. This position was perfect. I kept normal business hours, which allowed me to start fertility treatments.

After our third attempt with in vitro fertilization, (IVF), injections included, we were pregnant with twins. We were so excited. Then, during the six- week checkup, the doctor tells us that we lost one of the twins. We were devastated but, the doctor said the other baby is growing strong and we even heard the heartbeat. We were so happy; life was going great again, both personally and professionally.

The flight attendant that I flew with, that drank like a fish, and smoked, and talked like a sailor, moved out of her boyfriend's apartment and moved in to an apartment closer to me, only a few minutes away. We soon both learned we had a hunger to know more about God and Jesus.

I told her about my pregnancy and loss and we both cried and prayed together that this baby would grow strong and healthy. In my ninth week, we found out we were having a boy. What an exciting time for everyone; this was going to be my parents' first grandchild, too. I was excited to soon be a mother.

Life was exciting. During my twelfth week, the infertility doctor said it was time to switch doctors. *Why would I want to switch doctors?* This came as a shock and a surprise to us.

The doctor said that we had passed the danger point and that it was time for her to help others like us. She provided me a list of doctors who could assist for the duration of my pregnancy and through to the delivery. I was shocked.

"What do you mean?" I just couldn't make sense of it. "Don't you help with delivery?"

"No," she said with a clinical tone, "we only get you pregnant and once you have a viable pregnancy, we no longer assist you."

I left my appointment with a list of high-risk pregnancy doctors. I was scared and puzzled; the doctor reassured me that everything was going to be ok, but I wasn't as confident.

I found a great group of doctors on Long Island where we were living, and the hospital was not too far; that helped to some degree. During my fifth month, I decided to go back on the line; changing my work status would free me up sooner to stay at home for the baby. I did this so I would not have to work until my ninth month, on the ground.

My time at work was just about fulfilled before maternity leave when I went in for my check up. The doctor immediately said to me that the baby was too small for his age. He measured my belly carefully and began to press into my stomach firmly.

"You're going to hurt the baby!" I screamed as his hand pressed into my belly. The doctor smiled and reassured me that, everything was alright. About then, the baby started moving in my belly, in response to the firm intrusion.

The doctor said that I would be able to make a video of the baby, for the family – now, that sounded exciting to me.

The nurses made an appointment for the following week.

I was five-and-a-half months pregnant when I asked for line duty so that I could enjoy my pregnancy. My manager was thrilled for me and easily agreed. I was required to serve one trip. I did my one trip to satisfy the requirements, a simple turn around; it was quick and uneventful.

The next day, my former boss asked if I could fill in for someone in the operations side of In-Flight. It seemed like a simple request, and I agreed. Before I knew it, my shift was over. My husband had just come in from a long flight. The timing of our schedules was perfect; we finished at the same time, and, together, we walked out the door to get on the bus to the employee parking lot.

It began to rain; we both looked at each other at the same time, and agreed to stop and pick up Chinese for dinner, on the way home. Just then, the rain began coming down stronger and the LIE (Long Island Expressway), was jammed-packed with cars.

We were just two exits away from home when, all of a sudden, a driver in a Volvo began to hydroplane and hit my side of the shuttle van we were riding in.

We began to do 360's; cars were moving out of our way as rapidly as they could. We finally came to a stop, and the man who made impact, jumped out of his car and could see that I was pregnant. He ran back to his car and called an ambulance. Only in New York, the cars were taking turns going around our cars; no one stopped to offer help.

Just then, an ambulance arrived and asked if we need help. My husband explained that I wasn't bleeding. The ambulance driver was hospitable, but with no sense of urgency.

"We could get you out of here fast and find out if everything is alright," he offered,

My husband said that we should go to our doctors, instead.

"It's really close, or we can just go home, we are the next exit," he was calm, but indecisive.

In the end, we went home and I called my doctor, who asked if there was any bleeding or pain. I said "no." The doctor said, "I'm sure it's nothing, but, I am going to change your sonogram from Thursday to tomorrow."

Relieved, I thanked him, and, hung up. I felt fine that night, just a little shaken. As life would have it, my husband got called out again and left the next morning for a trip. *At least I know he will be home early*, I thought as he headed out. My husband called later and said he wouldn't be coming home until later that evening.

I went to the radiologist that afternoon with my VCR tape, ready for copying to give to family. I was called back right away within minutes, ready as ever to begin. I was undressed and on the table when something seemed to go wrong.

The technician turned on the machine and all of the sudden, I heard a gasp. The one lady insisted the machine was not working.

"We are going to change rooms, this machine is not working," she said with an odd, crisp clip. "Please put your clothes on, we will be back in a minute."

I ask if I could see the monitor.

"It's not working," the technician replied, and quickly exited the room.

I anxiously got dressed and the doctor came into the room. He slams his glasses on the table along with my file and begins to ask me, "is anyone with you? "

"No," I answered, having come alone, while Tom was on a flight.

And then he told me that I should go home and wait until my husband is home to call. I demand to know what is going on.

The doctor spurts out, "This is what happens when you do infertility!"

"What?" I asked with increasing concern.

The doctor blurts out in response, "your baby is dead." He picks up his glasses, and the file, and walks out of the room.

I was stunned at everything that had just transpired. I began to sob, to the point of hysteria. One of the nurses came in and shortly after, "I'm sorry, but we need the room."

She escorted me to the bathroom so that I could continue my sobbing and pull myself together. I was at the point of no return. I was heaving and on the cold, bathroom floor. I must have been in there for a while when I heard a knock on the door. I could not move toward the door or respond to the knock.

The receptionist pops open the door and explained that people needed to use the restroom. She helped me up to the broom closet, again, so I could continue my sobbing and grieving, out of sight. To this day, I can still smell the ammonia and cleaning fluids.

I could not stop crying; I could hear my heartbeat in my ears. My head fell to my chest and I called upon the only one I knew who would come to my rescue.

"Jesus, if you are real, please help me; I can't do this!"

I remember kneeling on the floor; the brooms had fallen on my back, and my eyes burning from my mascara and the salt from my tears. My chest was heaving and I fell onto the floor, unable to hold myself up any longer. Then the most amazing thing happened.

I could hear a voice say, "WHEN YOU HURT, I HURT, WHEN YOU CRY I CRY!"

This seemed to make me spiral out of control even more.

"I can't do this!" I screamed right into the broom closet.

The voice says more firmly, "I WILL NEVER LEAVE YOU, I LOVE YOU!"

Just then, the door flings open and the receptionist is looking down at me in disgust. She pulled me up and informs me, "I have the elevator for you."

I tried to pull myself together, but could not stop sobbing. I could tell the place was full of people with all different injuries and needs, but I never looked up. As I approached, the elevator door opened and the receptionist pushed me into the elevator.

I looked up just a bit to get my bearings, and I see this older man pushing himself into the wall of the elevator, avoiding eye contact with me. The elevator door closed and I am finally muffling my cries as best as I can. I try to hold my breath, thinking this would hold in my cries, instead, I feel my hand being lifted. I turned to the side to see who or what was moving my hand and my eyes lock eyes with the sweetest little boy, in the elevator with his mom. The boy begins to kiss my hand and the floodgates of tears come pouring out. The mother says to me, "sorry," and looks away to avoid eye contact with me.

"No, I am sorry," I offer, ashamed of my tears, imagining my appearance. The elevator doors open after an eternity, and everyone makes a quick exit, glad to be away from my obvious pain.

I reached down into my purse to get my car keys out, and the realization that I can't drive home, hits me. I'm not sure how to get home, and I haven't the foggiest recollection of where I parked the car.

As I began to look around, I called out to "Jesus please help me!"

I turned to the front of the building and standing in front of me is this lovely older woman with one of those tight perms, sensible shoes, and a purse to match. She looks at me and smiles and asks, "Do you believe in Jesus?"

I shake my head up and down. The tears and sobs come out again, with a full flow to the point I can feel my back begin to hurt.

The woman holds me and says, "Everything is going to be all right."

She kisses my cheek, just as a mom would and repeats it over and over, "Everything is going to be all right."

I noticed my breathing becoming less intense and I remember telling her that I was scared to drive home, and I don't even know where my car was parked.

I reached in my purse to get a tissue to wipe the large amount of snot and tears that was smeared on both of us, at this point. I dropped my keys. I bent down to pick them up, and the woman was gone. Just like that – gone. I looked in all directions, but could not see her. I clicked my car key remote, in hopes of finding my car, and, that is when I discovered that my car was parked right next to where I was standing. How could that be?

I opened the car door. The wave of emotions began to envelope me again. *Is this really happening?* Is my sweet, precious baby boy dead?

I opened and closed my eyes, hoping to wake up, as if I were in a bad dream in bed. I turned on the a/c and begin to shake; I closed my eyes and the next thing I knew,

I was pulling into my driveway. To this day, I do not know how I got home, only that the drive without any traffic takes a good twenty minutes and I have to cross over two highways from where I lived. God sent an angel to help me on my way.

As I got out of the car, I realized I needed to get my husband from the airport. I quickly called my office mate, the flight attendant who smoked and drank like a sailor. I told her everything that had happened. She asked if I wanted her to come over, but I declined; all I wanted was my husband.

He had just landed from a flight, so I asked if she would go to another gate to look for my husband. She went looking for him, but he wasn't there. I was very disappointed. I really wanted my husband to be home. It seemed, just as I hang up the phone, my husband opened the door. Apparently, I was numb for hours, and hours had passed. I was standing in the entrance of our home for several hours. I was so glad he was finally home to share the burden.

My husband opened the door and I immediately fell into his arms and began to sob. I blurted out, "the baby is dead". Now, we are both sobbing on the front door stoop. He picks me up and consoles me in the best way he can, "We will try again; everything will be alright."

Soon after we were inside, we had to contact all of our family and friends, and people at our work. We both sobbed for hours, during the phone calls and after. My husband made me some tea to calm me, and then, he started to call the family. I wasn't ready to talk to anyone. I could not even get dressed. I just sat there on the couch with no sense of time. I simply could not stop crying, and I just sat there for hour upon hours.

My step-sons both called and I could hear the anguish in their voices. My mom, however, kept telling me about all of her issues and reassured me to "keep trying, it's not the end." It felt like the end to me. In fact, I'm not really sure what it felt like. I was just so numb.

I had to contact Delta and let them know. I got a mixed bag of responses. The administrator from Delta was very perfunctory, "I'm sorry for your loss. You only get two weeks off," and then she went on to give me the details of my new report time.

I contacted my boss from Human Resources, who was equally heartless and said nothing, not even to offer my position back. She just hung up after I told her my devastating news. My operations manager was just the opposite, offering me the moon and back, and all the sympathy and time I needed. I thought she was an angel.

My husband suggested it would be a good idea to get out of the house in New York and go visit his hometown. We would often stay there when we had long weekends, or if there was a football game. We both found that going there was like having a retreat; everything was calm and lovely and peaceful there.

As we made our preparations to leave, it hit me that I didn't know what I would wear. I could not fit in my regular clothes yet, and could not bear the thought of wearing maternity clothes. After all, I was no longer pregnant. I did not want to talk about being pregnant, let alone have anyone think I was pregnant, or ask to touch my belly.

We went out to dinner that night and my husband saw friends of his dining at the same restaurant. I was still numb, going through the motions. I wasn't ready to be out yet. To make matters worse, my husband's friend's wife asked me when I was due. It was my anger that began to unleash and overflow into a pool of tears. I ran into the bathroom, followed by the woman, telling me how truly sorry she was and that she never meant to hurt me. I apologized. I was still very raw. It was an innocent remark.

After pulling myself together, my husband remarked that we are in a small town and I need to handle things better. His comment undoes me, and I tell him he should be thankful there were no knives near me. In that painful moment, I realized I was truly on my own with my pain and my grief.

During our time away, we went to visit my mother-in-law in the nursing home. She had suffered a stroke, and unfortunately, had an accident during her physical therapy, which had left her permanently paralyzed on her right side. My mother- in-law was a nurse for more than fifty years. She would say she birthed most everyone in town and had seen their backside, as well.

Nurses are so very important, but some can be the hardest natured-people, no doubt from all they have seen and experienced in their careers. I realized I was very sensitive to what was being said to me but, the sting certainly cut right through me when my mother- in- law said, "I'm so thankful my boy had children from his first marriage."

She delivered this statement right in front of my step son, and to my husband in front of me, in my pain. The sting was real, but the lesson was well received, from this moment, I realized I could never count on anyone or anything where only God can heal.

Chapter Nine

WHO'S THAT
KNOCKING THE WALL

Devastated over the loss of my baby, I decided to keep flying the line. I thought if I kept working it would take my mind off things, besides, there is something to say about flying to places where most people are dreaming about. I picked up trips that would take me far away. My former boss from operations asked if I would like my job back, and even gave me the option to fill in a couple of days a week. That suited me just fine. I worked any time I could, either on the ground or in the air, to fill the void and hide the pain.

I had picked up a trip to Brussels, thinking this was a perfect time to go. What a mistake it was - very cold and rainy on and off. As I was heading out of the hotel, I realized I had forgotten my umbrella, so I walked to the concierge desk and asked if there was an extra umbrella I could use. The man smiled and said, "You will be a walking advertisement for us." The umbrella was as big as me, and had the hotel name emblazoned on the broad umbrella top, but it did the trick.

I walked around the old city and came across the famous statue of the mermaid. I asked this man walking by if he would mind taking my picture next to the statue. He smiled and said that he would love to. I struck a pose, and he began to shoot the camera, using up almost the entire roll of film in the camera. He handed back the camera and meekly apologized. He commented that he was not familiar with using such a fancy camera.

"It's a throw away,' I said, as I throw the camera back into my purse.

I look up to see that I am directly in front of a kid's toy store. I decide to go in and buy something cheerful. As I look around the shop, I can't help but notice the wonderful wood craftsmanship. The toys are not the same as the ones found in an American department store; these items are probably what our great grandparents enjoyed during their childhood.

The woman asked me if I was buying for a boy or a girl, and I said that I didn't know. She squealed with delight and flashed me a broad grin.

"This is the best thing to get," she excitedly pulled over a toy that was obviously a favorite, "every child loves these."

It was an old-fashioned wooden clown. When you push the buttons on the side of the toy, the clown is propelled to motion in a circle.

I know that it's perplexing, why I would buy a toy after losing a baby? A friend of mine said that the best thing to do to help you obtain your dream is to visualize what you want, and for me, that was to have a baby. She encouraged me to do whatever it takes to make that thought a reality; *why not,* I thought.

I'm standing in front of this genuine toy shop that has been around since the 1700's, and my dream is to have a baby, and her encouragement came to mind. I desperately wanted another chance at having a baby.

As the clerk was wrapping up the toy, it did not help to visualize myself with a child. I'm sure my friend's advice was sound, but, in fact, it made me feel worse. I kept going over everything that had happened to me in regards to losing the babies and I became very angry at the entire situation. I couldn't comprehend how I had accepted Christ into my life and nothing good, or should I say nothing that I desired, had come to fruition.

As the rain started to come down a little harder, who should I see, but Lillian, my dear, sweet, crazy, Evangelical flight attendant, who I once had shared some deep Jesus conversations.

I screamed across the street, "Lillian!"

Lillian turned around, along with a friend with whom she was walking. I waved my hands wildly, and ran across the street.

I just blurt out, 'We need to talk!"

Clearly, this was not a friendly tone because the woman Lillian had been walking with politely said an immediate "goodbye."

I tried to muster a smile, but it did not work.

"Have you eaten?" Lillian asked.

I shake my head no, hoping she did not ask because she had heard my stomach rumbling. I had been walking around all day and had not eaten anything; I could hear it making gurgling noises.

"I'm starved!"I confessed.

She pointed to the restaurant behind her and explained it was a great restaurant, known for their tomato soup and mussels. I was quickly agreeable to go in and find something for dinner.

"How funny that here we are eating mussels in Brussels," I managed to quip, quickly turning to Lillian with a more serious matter.

"I can see something is bothering you," Lillian said, as more of a question than a statement. "What is going on with this Jesus stuff? I asked"

"What do you mean, this 'Jesus stuff?'?" Lillian asked.

"I am very angry with what has happened to me, and where is this God you shared with me?"

I was perplexed and deeply wounded. "I was expecting to be treated like royalty," I protested my circumstances. "How could I lose the babies when I'm a believer? I want answers as to what is going on."

"I don't have answers, especially to questions I can never answer," she said as if to brush me off. Then firmly added, "You need to have a conversation with God."

I looked at her as if she was crazy, which I might add happened often.

"What am I supposed to do, pick up the phone and ask for God?" I said, not understanding what she was implying.

"No," she said calmly, "you just need to sit down and talk to God, just like you and I are talking right now."

"That's it?" I ask incredulously.

"Yes," she replied, "and, don't stop reading your bible."

'I love you, but you are clearly missing a screw," I half chuckle. "If that is all you do, then everyone would be doing it."

I remind her about 'in the old days' when the Holy Temple was around and how the head priest was the only person who could talk to God, and if he had issues (sins), God would annihilate even him.

"What do you have to lose?" she prodded me to no end. "Try it."

We finished our meal, gave each other hugs, and agreed to keep in touch. We both went to our different hotels. As I was walking back to my hotel, I thought how fortunate I was to stumble upon Lillian, and have a great dinner on top of that. I entered the hotel and gave back the umbrella to the concierge and went straight to my room. I was freezing and took a hot shower. As I came out of the shower, I briskly towel-dried my hair. I looked up at the ceiling and rather awkwardly said, "God it's me." I assumed we did not need introductions. I started speaking about all the things that were going on in my life. I wanted to know why he was not doing anything to help me.

"Where are you?" I heard myself ask aloud. "Why aren't you doing anything?" Not realizing my voice had escalated and I was no longer speaking in a normal tone, but screaming.

I hear this loud knock on the shared wall in my hotel room. The person next door was screaming for me to 'shut up.' I could not believe that happened, then the phone rang; it was the operator asking me if everything was alright, inquiry if she needed to send up security! Embarrassed, I apologized and said I would lower the TV and keep it down. I hung the phone on the receiver. *This is not getting me anywhere,* I thought to myself.

I dried my hair, set my alarm, and opened up the bible from the night stand drawer. As I was reading, it seemed that the stories were all the same. I could not concentrate. I looked over at the clock and was surprised at the time. My pick up was scheduled six hours away.

I started dozing off to sleep and began to cry. Everything that I had lost quickly flooded my mind. Through the tears, I kept asking God, "Where were you?"

I kept looking up at the ceiling, as if the answers would be plastered there. Then I heard this soft voice ask me, "You want to know where I was?" The voice continued to say,"I was with you everywhere." I knew it was God because the things that I was hearing only God could know.

"Do you remember when you and your sister where swimming?"God asked.

I had forgotten all about that time, and God kept reminding me of other times in my life of things that happened to me. And, then he asked, "Do you not remember when you found out our sweet baby died? I was there holding you in my arms telling you, I love you, and I even sent my angels to tell you how much I love you!"

I could not stop crying, God had been with me my entire life, and I never realized He was there. Then, like a floodgate, the Lord showed me how he had been trying to reach me, even when I was younger. I became angry thinking *if God had told me about Jesus earlier my life would have been different.*

> I knew you before I formed you in your mother's womb. Before you were born I set you apart and appointed you as my prophet to the nations."
>
> Jeremiah 1:5

The Lord asked me, "Do you not remember when you and your mother were watching TV?"

I had forgotten all about that time, too. I can still see it as if it was happening right now. My mom was wearing her navy dress, hair and nails perfectly polished. Mom had on nylons and heels, along with pearls; she was smoking a cigarette and we were watching the TV.

The man on the TV was Billy Graham. I was listening intently and everything he said sounded perfect. Mr. Graham was convicted, convincing viewers, too,

"The only way to true happiness and peace is through Jesus Christ."

I turned to my mom and said, "We should do that!"

"We are Jewish; we don't do that." My mom turned off the TV and started to work on preparing dinner. The subject never came up again, and I had forgotten all about the incident until that rainy, fateful day.

> So do not fear, for I am with you; do not be dismayed, for I am your God. I will strengthen you and help you; I will uphold you with my righteous right hand.
>
> Isiah 41:10

> And surely I am with you always, to the very end of the age.'
>
> Mathew 28:20

Chapter Ten

FREE GIFT
WITHOUT PURCHASE

I had entered the deep abyss of my life. I could not understand how all of this could be happening to me. I had a constant dread and anger in me that was not going away. My friend Kim, who had worked with me in the office and on the line, suggested we go to the Joyce Meyer's Women's conference. The year was 1997.

I was still grieving in my heart. My husband did not know what to do for me, anymore, and thought I should go. "It can't hurt, besides, the tickets have been paid for," he encouraged me.

I called Kim and agreed to go and packed my bags, half-heartedly. Kim had already left and told me to call her when I landed. The plane ride was fast and uneventful. I called her when I landed and asked her which hotel we were staying in. Her reply nearly knocks me on the floor. She tells me she was 'working on it.'

"What?" I blurted out. 'Are you kidding me?"

Several thousand people were coming to this conference, how could she be so ill-prepared?

'Well, I thought I could just get a hotel room when we arrived," she said sheepishly.

"I'm going back to New York," I said with displeasure.

"Please, just give me a minute," she said, "I think I have a room for us, which is walking distance to the conference."

"That's better; well, fantastic, really," I say in a calmer voice.

"You don't mind if we share our room?" she asks hesitantly.

"Of course not," I said, happy to hear we had a room at all. "We are flight attendant's, and years ago, that was the norm - sharing rooms," I said.

The conference was in St. Louis, MO, near the downtown area. I jumped on the train and got off the exit, close to the hotel. The hotel was walking distance of ten minutes to the conference. I met Kim in the lobby of the hotel and quickly rode the elevator to place my bags in the room. As it turned out, we were sharing the room with three other ladies.

One African American lady was from the Midwest and the two other women were Hispanic, from the East Coast. We all hugged each other and off we went to the conference. My friend Lillian was also going to join us the next day.

The conference was powerful, inspiring, and amazing. I had never experienced anything similar; to be near so many believers increased my faith and my hunger to know more of who Jesus is or was!

That night, they had an alter call and I gave my life to Christ with such a deep conviction that I could not stop crying. My friend Kim said that she wanted to invite me to go, but by the time she turned to me, I was halfway down the aisle, running to the center of the floor. I did not see her until after the alter call. We were given a little book about who we are in Christ. I cherished that book and read it till the pages were thin and falling out of the book.

They had musicians that sang such beautiful music it made me weep. For the first time, I heard the beautiful hymn "His eye is on the Sparrow." I was deeply touched.

> Look at the birds of the air; they do not sow or reap or store away in barns, and yet your heavenly Father feeds them. Are you not much more valuable than they?
>
> Mathew 6:26

That evening was truly the first time I felt that unconditional love that only God can give. That is when I heard Linda Pepper sing the song, "Honey if you knew what I knew you would be shouting, too." I thought to myself, I wish everyone knew what I knew about Jesus. The last day of the conference, my friend got tickets for this thing called 'breakout sessions.'

This was my first Women's conference or any type of Christian event.

I did not understand, nor was I prepared for what was ahead at the Saturday afternoon sessions.

"We are going to these breakout sessions," Kim said,"I signed us up for the 'Free Gift of Tongues class.

" I must admit the only thing I heard was 'Free Gift'. As we were walking to the room for the break out session, my mind was on our flight home. I wondered how much room was in my bag. I really didn't want to have to check my bag, so that was important to me.

We waited in the line forming to get into the room, when someone announced in the hall, "If you have not accepted Christ, please go through the doors on your left; everyone else, go the doors on the right."

My friend and I walked through the doors on the right when this lady stopped me and asked, "Have you accepted Christ?" I tell her "Yes!" I'm sporting a wide, satisfying grin to prove it. My friend nods in confirmation, and next thing I know, I am separated from my friend and taken away with the woman.

This woman asks me, "Would you like your free gift of tongues?"

I show her my ticket and my bag, and ask her, "Would the gift fit in my bag?"

The woman falls over laughing, while I'm marveling at the possibilities of this 'Free Gift.' "Wow, this gift must be larger than I thought."

Just then, my friend comes up to me and asked, "Did you get the gift?"

I shake my head no and she said, "Me either."

The next thing I know, she turns to the side and is talking with someone else. A man walked up to me. He was one of the musicians who played guitar and sang in the praise band. He asked me,"Would you like the free gift of tongues?'

At this point, I am frustrated and say again, "YES, but will it fit in my bag?"

With a warm smile, the man explained to me, "It's not that kind of gift."

"Have you made Jesus, your Lord?"

"Yes."I smiled.

"Have you confessed your sins?" he pressed in.

"Nobody told me about that, "I admitted. And, then, I started confessing my sins – out loud, to him.

"NO! Don't tell me - tell a priest or someone else, but, not me!" he seemed adamant about it.

So, I told him that I am Jewish and I'm trying to figure what is going on with this Jesus stuff. He smiled back and asked,"Is your friend also Jewish?" as he pointed to Kim.

I tell him "No."

Frustrated, I walked away, and that is when I noticed several women down on the floor; some were shaking, and others were just lying on the floor with their eyes closed. The Flight Attendant in me kicked in and I ran up to one of the ladies and began to shake her asking, "Are you alright?"

I fervently looked to see if she was breathing, when all of a sudden, my friend pulled me up by the shirt, and grabbing some of my hair, said to me, "They are slain in the spirit; leave them alone!"

I was quite shocked. For all of you Pentecostal women, who a roaring with laughing at this point, it's downright scary to see such a thing, when you have never encountered anything like this in your life. The only time I have seen something similar was in a movie, and people were dropping like flies, due to illness.

As my friend was screaming at me to leave the lady alone, another lady with a beehive hairdo walked up and asked me, "Were you able to get the gift of tongues?"

I looked her straight in the eye and said to her, "Look," as I point to my suitcase, "does it look like I have the gift?"

The woman smiled so patiently and sweetly, and said, "The gift of tongues is not a gift with purchase; it's the ability to speak in God's language, and, it's completely free."

"I speak Hebrew, and that is God's language," I said, rather irritated by what seemed like a lot of nonsense.

The lady calmly asks me to extend my hands to hers. I extend my hands, like I'm readying for a manicure with Madge.

"Close your eyes," she commands me.

Compliantly, I closed my eyes.

"Now, keep saying the name of Jesus," she softly instructs me.

I do this at least four or five times. Then she asks me to open my mouth. I open my mouth, and then she commands me to 'speak.'

My mouth is open and nothing is coming out. The lady reassures me, "It's on the tip of your tongue, keeping practicing, and you will get it."

I walked out, without my 'free gift.'

My friend immediately saw me and asked, "Anything?"

I shake my head no. We hug each other and, both at the same time, we said, "this is what we needed."

We both laughed and begin to show each other the assortment of tapes, cassettes and books we both purchased; neither with a 'free gift' in our bags. We agreed that it was a great time we had enjoyed at the conference.

We hugged a final time and said our goodbyes.

Chapter Eleven

WILL I SEE MY BABIES IN HEAVEN?

The women's conference came to a close and I jumped on the train back to the airport. I got to the gate just in time and waited for my name to be called. I heard the agent call my name, and when she handed me my ticket, I discovered, a first class seat assigned to my name; what a great ending.

The plane was not full, and I was seated next to this elderly man. As the plane pushed off from the gate, I could feel myself dozing off. All of a sudden, I felt a sharp pain in my leg. As I look down at my leg to see what the heck is going on, I see the flight attendant, having just kicked me, still hovering over me.

I look at her with a sharp look, to which she returned the same expression, and with a low, stern voice, you were crying in your sleep. The gentleman sitting next to me moved to an empty seat. The flight attendant asked if I needed a drink. I apologize profusely to both of them and tell the flight attendant that that had never happened before. Feeling embarrassed, I retrieved my bible to read.

The Flight attendant who kicked me asked, "Did you go to the Joyce Meyer's Conference?"

I smiled and said yes, after discovering that she had, too, we both agreed, it was awesome. It seemed like we were going to drive back to New York then fly, after a full forty minutes on the runway, the plane finally took off. I begin to fall asleep again, as I heard the engine roar. I kept hearing that verse that was mentioned in the conference, over and over again in my head.

Every knee will bow and confess that Jesus is Lord and those who do will enter into heaven. Romans 14:11

After about eight or ten loops of this, and the realization hit me - my babies never said that special prayer, or confessed Jesus as their Lord. My heart sank thinking that I would not see them in heaven. I was never taught about heaven. I can sincerely say as a Jew, the subject is never brought up, in fact, if you ask any Jew, the response will be the same - when you're dead your dead. Kind of like the term "ashes to ashes, dust to dust." You only get one life and that all folks.

I called out to God right in that moment on the plane; will *I ever see my precious babies?*

That is when I saw the most amazing thing. I was no longer on the airplane, but in Heaven. I was supernaturally transported, or something, and standing in front of the most beautiful waterfall. I could smell the water; it was sweet, and the ripples in the water and flowers were all swaying rhythmically to the music. The music was something I had never heard before. The melody was like harps and pipes and all sorts of wind instruments in harmony. Every time the flowers swayed, a new song was being played. It smelled so good, and the temperature was perfect - not too hot, yet a constant, soft breeze with a light, heavenly scent.

As I looked down, I noticed I was standing on these large gem stones. I was surprised that they were all sorts of stones, rubies, diamonds, sapphires, and emeralds. The stones were jagged and you could see their diverse dimensions as if you were looking through a prism. I was afraid to move, fearing that I would cut my feet. With a bit of apprehension, I moved my one foot ever so slowly, ensuring not to cut my feet on any of the jagged edges. When I pressed down on the stone with my toes, something astonishing happened. The stones went flat and did not hurt my feet, in spite of the raw edges. With a sigh of relief, I looked up and saw a tree like one you might see in Africa. It was if I had been teleported to another destination; certainly, I was no longer seated on the airborne plane.

Under the tree was a lion that had huge paws and its fur was waving in the wind. The craziest thing was that the lion had been playing with a dog; they were both jumping and licking each other. I kept thinking that at any minute, the dog was going to be eaten, but they kept on joyfully playing.

I turned my head and I saw a man standing next to me, he is wearing a white robe. I look to him and then to the ground, and asked him, "am I dead?"

"No, but you are in heaven, and, "we are going to be late!" he said.

"Late for what," I ask.

"Don't you want to praise Jesus?" he asked me with excitement.

"Yes!" I shouted joyously.

The next thing I know is that I am in this tower, and I can hear a choir singing and voices giving praises to God and Jesus. It was the most beautiful sound I have ever heard in my life. I could not identify all the instruments.

A man had instruments on his body, and when the wind would blow, a sound was made, and a choir would sing.

I asked the man what denomination is this? He looked amused and said, "There are no denominations here."

I looked to my right and saw two thrones. Trying to see first throne, I nearly fell over because of its enormity. It looked like something the jolly green giant would use. Next to that throne was another throne, not as ornate or big, but it was also made of gold and had a large red velvet seat stuffed with a million feathers. I looked all around and no one was there so, I jumped on the smaller throne and let out a gleeful sound and the red velvet seat slipped out from the pressure of my weight, and went over my head; I could not stop laughing.

I slid down from the throne with every intention to do it again, but, that's when I noticed that I was not alone. Out of the corner of my eye, I saw a man standing next to a huge window. As I walked closer towards the window, I could see the back of Jesus. He had on the most brilliant white gown, it sparkled and looked so soft. He was on his knees, weeping. I began to cry, too. I was looking out the window he was looking out and I kept seeing fiery arrows coming towards him.

At each arrow, I ducked and He said, "Those arrows are every word that the people speak. I can hear the pleas as the arrows are whizzing by."

"Every word you speak, I hear." He gently said.

As soon as an arrow comes to him, he sends angels and arrows back. Then I saw something that startled me even more. Some of the arrows that were whizzing by continued flying, and then I saw the hole in Jesus hand when he raised it to hold back the angels going out the window.

"What's going on?" I asked.

"People are cursing me and others," he wept as he said the words.

I began to cry with him, and thought of the things I wish I had never said. I lowered my head.

As I began to lift my head up, I heard a young man calling, "Mom!"The young man kept screaming, "Mom!'

I looked around and realized I was no longer in the tower with Jesus. I was standing on a street. There in front of me was a huge wall of water and as I looked through I could see a field with green grass. I heard the young man again scream, 'Mom!"

I turned to see if anyone could help the young man. I walked up to him. He looked to be about 20 years old; he was wearing khaki pants with a blue button- down oxford shirt. His hair color was light brown and his eyes were brown.

I called over to him, "Hi."

He smiled at me and said, "Hi."

I told him my name and he said, "I know who you are; you're my mom!

"I am Noah Riley, and he used his finger to point to the car seat that was next to him, and softly, he says, this is Zachary."

I nearly fell over with the shock of his words. *Could it be?* I dared to think.

Those were the names I gave our twins. Every baby I lost, I had named them all - all five of them. I reached out to hug him but, he tells me, "not yet."

He moved back into a field.

There were hundreds of kids playing, I could hear laughing and singing. The kids were playing on a large field, and there was every kind of toy and playground equipment the eye could see. It smelled so fresh, if you have ever been around kids who sweat, it smells just like wet dog, instead, it smelled of fresh cut grass and fragrant flowers. The temperature was perfect, and there was a warm cool breeze. My heart melted at seeing all the children playing happily.

Just as I tried to walk on the field, the plane touched down, and woke me.

For years, it puzzled me why Jesus was not on the throne. Then, one day in church, the pastor said something that reminded me just how much God loves us. He said, "Do you know that God cannot sit down on the throne because he is interceding on our behalf and, busy listening to all of our pleas."

So, if you ever wonder if God is listening to you, the answer is yes, He is, and He is also doing something constantly on your behalf, as well. Choose your words carefully, my friends. I know I am equally guilty of this but, remember there is life or death in the tongue, I remind you to chose life.

> This day I call the heavens and the earth as witnesses against you that I have set before you life and death, blessing and curses. Now choose life, so that you and your children may live and that you may love the Lord your God, listen to his voice, hold fast to him. For the Lord is your life and he will give you many years in the land he swore to give to your father Abraham, Isaac and Jacob.
>
> Deuteronomy 30:19-20

Chapter Twelve

HOLY WHO?

I return to our home in New York, eager to share with my husband the great time I had experienced. I showed him all of the books, and cassette and VCR tapes full of great teaching material I had purchased. I don't know where to begin with all the things I saw and experienced.

My husband smiled sweetly, and then shared that we might be moving in the near future.

"What? Where? Why?" I was full of questions and my emotions were spinning. He explained he would know more by the end of the month. I asked where we would be moving to, and he speculated, "Maybe Atlanta."

"Atlanta?" I'm stunned, "We can't move there! We don't know anyone or have any family there!"

I knew it was futile to resist, so I continued to barrage him with questions, "When would we move? Are you sure'?"

My husband confirmed the move would be in the next month or two.

Then, all I could think of was the logistics, "Are you crazy, we can't move during Thanksgiving. Besides, we just renovated the entire house from the basement to the loft!" I was not happy about this at all, and searching for ways to protest.

And, exactly two months later, my husband broke the news to me, "I have to transfer to Atlanta in December and we have to do the move now, or the airlines won't pay for it!"

"I can't get my transfer in that fast," my head was reeling. "What about all of our stuff, and the car." Atlanta is one of the most senior bases. I can't hold an international line, let alone get a position in the office. I was concerned what my future career would look like, too.

My husband transferred into Atlanta ahead of me. He was living at a hotel and I was living in New York with no furniture or car. In the transition, I went to live with my cousin Marilyn for a month.

I was able to get my transfer to Atlanta scheduled for January and was not scheduled the last week of December through the first week of January, in order to get everything in order for our final move. As soon as I arrived, we began to look for a house to rent unsure if we would be staying long in Atlanta.

Our realtor was very funny; he knew nothing about the area in which we were looking to buy. We had been looking at houses all afternoon, and, from the last house we looked at, I thought we were going from worse to terrible. The look of despair was evident on our faces. Then, the realtor announced he was not at all sure about the next property we were scheduled to see.

"What do you mean?" my husband asks suspiciously.

The realtor explained that using MapQuest, the search for the address returned no results. The realtor excused himself to call his boss. "Maybe, she can help us," he assured us as he jumped out of the car, now parked in front of someone's house.

My husband and I had just begun reading Kenneth and Gloria Copeland's devotional, along with the bible, and he suggests we say a prayer. We say a quick prayer, hoping for the best. All of the sudden a man comes out of the house that we parked in front of and asked, "Are you all lost?"

My husband tells him our predicament. The man smiles and tells us that he and his wife just placed an offer on a house in town and he just found out their bid was a success. The man then told us that he was putting his house up for sale. We tell him that we only want to rent for a year because we are not sure what will happen at Delta.

And, here is the best part of this story: the man explained to us that the house we were standing in front of would soon be vacant. The house that he and his wife just bought is sitting vacant, with no one living in it, and then he wanted to know if we could move in within two weeks. This was good news.

"We would like to see the place first," my husband said.

"Of course," the man said, as he motioned to us to follow him. We walked in and immediately knew it was better than perfect. Meanwhile, the realtor learned the listing we were searching for was no longer available. We laughed at our situation and how God provided just what we were looking for at the right time.

We moved into the house within two weeks, find a great church, and meet our new neighbors. I shared my encounter with God with my new neighbor, and she asked me if I had been baptized?

"No," I tell her, and she retorts sharply, "You could go to hell."

'What?' I ask incredulously, "Nobody said anything about getting baptized, let alone I could go to hell." I ran home and asked my husband if he was baptized? His response nearly killed me.

"Yes when I was a baby," he said. I tell him the conversation with our neighbor to which he replied, "You need to talk to someone." "I'm thinking to myself *aren't you a someone?*

This is urgent, but my trip for work is leaving in three hours, and I will be gone for three days. In my mind I keep hearing 'going to hell.' I am completely unnerved that I was not informed I could go to hell! My stress level has begun to hit the roof, when I start to think of a million ways I could die, and I haven't even left the house. I have no doubt my odds will increase greatly as soon as I start to leave for work! My bags are packed and I tell my husband that I'm going to church. He was taken aback and asked, "Why?"

My reply was short." I don't want to go to hell." To which my husband responded, "Have a safe trip."

That afternoon I stop at the church we have already been attending. I am in full uniform and ask to speak with the associate pastor. The young man comes out and I just blurt out, "I'm Jewish and I've accepted Christ but, I need to get baptized right now!'

The associate pastor seems stunned and tries to slow me down, "You first must be approved by sessions then you can be baptized." Not to be deterred, I ask him, "Where is that in the bible?" "It's not in the bible," he says, stammering a bit, "but, it's part of our bylaws."

Just then the head pastor walked out of his office and I walk up to him and said, "I need to be baptized *right now!*"

To our amazement, the head pastor agrees, and quickly said, "Okay."

The associate pastor is more resistant, "We can't do that; she needs to be approved by sessions!"

"He's right," said the head pastor in agreement.

I was getting upset. The head pastor shook his shoulders and left the room.

"If I die and go to hell, it's your entirely your fault!"I said to the associate pastor, pointing my finger at him. The associate pastor faces goes ash white as he asked me, "Have you accepted Christ?"

"Yes," I say firmly. The pastor then explained that the baptism is about the Holy Spirit, not my salvation.

"Who is the Holy Spirit?" I asked. "I only accepted Jesus."

"When you get baptized, the Holy Spirit lives in you," he explained.

"That doesn't tell me anything!" I was exasperated and more confused than ever.

"It's like this," he paused a minute, "God is the electricity and Jesus is the light switch, and the Holy Spirit is the light bulb."

I walk out confused, scared, and mad that I did not get 'the full package.'

I returned home and called my neighbor, the one who told me I was going to hell. My neighbor told me to meet her at the Baptist church she attends. Now I have less than an hour to get to work. I go to the church and meet the pastor of the Baptist church and tell him my dilemma.

"No worries," he said to me with a true twinkle of delight in his eye, I can baptize you right now."

"Woohoo, I'm not going to hell!" I exclaim. Everyone lets out a chuckle. I'm certain they weren't used to hearing that in the Baptist Church.

He leads me into the sanctuary where there is a giant dunking booth filled with water – but, it is green. The pastor invites me to "get in."

"Are you kidding me?" I asked, "I'm not getting in that disease-infested pool, besides, I am in my uniform."

I storm out of the church. I am in tears, numb, and driving at a snail's pace on the highway. People are honking at me to move over, but it doesn't even register - I keep hearing in my head, *you're going to hell.*

I sign in on my flight and tell the black, gay flight attendant on my flight what just happened. I have no idea why I told him; probably because he could see I was upset, and he truly had a kind face -, plus, he was wearing a ginormous cross.

He told me his mom was a prayer warrior and insisted that he would call her. "She will know what to do," he said.

I wasn't sure what a 'prayer warrior' was, but it sounded official. He came back and said excitedly, "My mom said I can do it!" We were both smiling and he began to tell me what we needed to do. First, he said we need to get water.

'Like holy water?" I asked. "Where do we get that?"

"No! My mom said any water would do.'

He literally took out a water bottle from his bag. I might add it was not even full, but, at this point, it beats the green water.

"I just need to sprinkle water on you and you have to confess that Jesus is Lord of your life and then you tell everyone you're a Christian," he explained.

The attendant held up the half full water bottle and asks, "Are you ready?"

That stopped me right there; not the half-full water bottle but, "who is *everyone?*"

"You know, your family, friends - those people." He said reassuringly.

I stop him right there. 'If I tell my family, they will disown me," I say honestly. He said it was similar to when he told his mom he was gay. I was devastated; I was not ready yet to tell my family friends. In spite of his enthusiasm, I was not yet ready, and we delayed the in-flight baptism.

I waited the allotted time at church and got approved by sessions. The associate pastor continuously told me to tell my family. I remember that I was reading my bible in bed and I heard that inner voice speak to me to call home.

"Why not, it's Friday night - Shabbat; they won't answer the phone, my mom had invited all her family and friends to the house for Shabbat meal, she will never pick up. Yes, this is a perfect time. I reasoned that this way I can say I called and check it off the list.

I picked up the phone and dialed my parents' home. After the third ring, I expected that the answering machine would pick up. Just as I was about to leave a message, I heard my Aunt Janet say, "hello."

What is she doing answering the phone? I think in shock.

I tell her it's me and I hear my mom's shoes clicking on the tile floor along with background noise from pots and pans. I tell my mom, "hello," and I just blurt out, without determination, "I am a Christian."

All of a sudden, the noise level went deafening silent. I asked my mom "do you have me on speaker phone?" I just hear a flat, weak, "YES," to which my mother added, "Wait, I'm getting your father!"

I pray, "Jesus, help me," under my breath. My dad picked up the phone and asked me, "Do you know what you are saying?"

I stood my ground and answered, "Yes."

"Do you know what this means?" he asks with a firm voice.

"Yes!" I respond.

We both cry and hang up.

Part of me was devastated yet, part of me was elated. My husband was on a trip but, I had my sweet dog, 'Pepper,' who just kept licking my tears. When my husband came home, I told him. That Sunday, we went to church. I told the associate pastor and explained to him how God kept telling me this bible verse, and that now, I was ready for baptism. I had, finally, told my family.

"I have come to bring fire on the earth, and how I wish it were already kindled! **50** But I have a baptism to undergo, and what constraint I am under until it is completed! **51** Do you think I came to bring peace on earth? No, I tell you, but division. **52** From now on there will be five in one family divided against each other, three against two and two against three. **53** They will be divided, father against son and son against father, mother against daughter and daughter against mother, mother-in-law against daughter-in-law and daughter-in-law against mother-in-law."

Luke 12:49-53

I found comfort and reassurance in the book of John. The Lord told me about the orphaned.

"I will not leave you as orphans, I will come to you."

John 14:18

I know this sounds crazy, but I didn't feel alone, in spite of the circumstances. The Lord kept pressing on me how he will never leave me nor forsake me, and I found peace in that. You will never, ever be alone when you put God first. To show how much God loves you and me, he gave us his one and only Son that who shall ever believe in him will NEVER EVER PERISH! This is a promise from God who never lies, and He will *always* be with you.

I know the LORD is always with me. I will not be shaken, for he is right beside me.

Psalm 16:8

Chapter Thirteen

TAKE THIS DESIRE AWAY

After the devastating loss of our twins and moving to Atlanta, I found another infertility doctor that was close to the airport, which made it extremely convenient to begin infertility treatments right away. At the time, I was working as an HR Supervisor in In-Flight International.

The doctors were just as professional and nice as the ones in New York. I felt very comfortable, and within two months, I was pregnant. I remember calling my mom right away; we both were overly elated. My husband came home from his trip and was ecstatic, as well. My husband said, "Wow, this time was a whole lot faster than last time. Remember, how I thought we should have called the boys Mercedes Benz?" I shake my head, and my husband said, "Looks like we have a Toyota on our hands." We both laughed and hugged each other.

I happily continued to work as this was all still new. My hours at work had amped up because of the new implementations to the flight attendant in-charge testing program. As a supervisor in that department, I was required to have all the certifications of those in my group.

I had scheduled my test date on Friday, thinking I could get out early that day. As I was about to leave my office, two flight attendants entered my office screaming at each other. I tell them that I am scheduled to take exam in fifteen minutes and ask them if they would like to come back or perhaps speak with someone else.

They did not want to leave, so I patiently listened to them both and heard them out. I asked them to record everything in writing and to put in detail any infractions they observed or were aware of. They both left my office with paper in hand.

I nearly sprinted to where the test was taking place. The room was packed, and I had to take a seat next to the prompter. The test started as soon as I took my seat. About half way through, I felt a stabbing pain, followed by strong cramps. I hurried through the test and ran to the bathroom. I noticed I was spotting and ran right to my office. I open the door and stepped on the papers the flight attendant's left under my door, nearly skating on them. I notified my boss that I was leaving to go to my doctor's office.

I drove as quickly as I could to the fertility doctor's office. I walked straight to the nurse's station, and she informed me, "He's not in today." I described what I had experienced. She dismissed my concerns and said that it was normal and not to worry. I asked her if I may see another doctor and was told that everyone had a full schedule and would not be able to squeeze me in. Hesitantly, I went home and put my feet up, and tried to relax.

Everything seemed to be fine, but I was on edge. Within the second month, during a check up, the doctor said, "The baby should have dropped at this point!"

Alarmed I asked, "What does that mean?"

Very Matter-of-factly, he said, "If the baby does not drop by the end of this week, we are going to have to do a D&C."

"No," I gasped. "I was told if I did that, I would probably never have children again because my fallopian tube would be shattered."

I quickly called my friend Vera. I met Vera through a bible study from Women's A Glow. Vera is a little older than me, on fire for the Lord, and had lead many bible studies; she is very insightful. I consider her to be a friend and a mentor. She immediately began to pray over me, over the telephone. She then encouraged me, "call everyone you know, including the 700 club!"

I called my friends from New York but, I did not know a lot of people in Atlanta. My husband and I had only been living in our new home for about three months. Vera gave me the number to call the 700 club. The women who answered the phone first inquired if I gave financially. I tell her no. I then get a dissertation on the importance of tithing, which lasted a good fifteen minutes. I tell her 'thank you' and I am about to hang up when she insisted, "Let's pray." Confused, I just sat quietly. When she said, "Amen," I hung up and felt worse than when I started.

I thought for a moment, *if I do sit ups, it would push the baby down*. Just then, the phone rings and it's my mother-in-law. She tells me it's not my fault, its nature's way of taking care of things and there is nothing you can do. She encouraged me to schedule the D&C right away to prevent any more damage. I went to work that morning and began to bleed, more than just spotting. I rushed over to the infertility doctors and underwent an emergency D&C.

I woke up from the procedure and my husband was standing over me, holding my hand. The doctor said, "Let's give it a few months and we will see from there." This is now the third time we had to make these phone

105

calls in less than a year and I was done. I did not want to talk to anyone. I contacted my manager and told her I wanted to go back to the line.

After a few days, my mom called and made a demand of me, "You are not to tell me ever again you are pregnant until you are over six months pregnant." I realized she was upset but, she had no clue how much that hurt me. My mother-in-law kept saying to me, "it's not good to keep putting this on your body." The ultimate heartache came when we went back to the fertility doctor who delivered the message that we needed to either adopt or give up, because there was no reason to keep trying. I hit the lowest emotional point until my husband agreed and said to me, "I don't want to do fertility anymore." I just hit rocked bottom.

I could no longer carry this burden, and I called out to God, 'Please take this desire out of me, if it's not meant to be. "My husband always says you find out the true nature of person when they are not able to obtain what they want.

I find it more interesting to hear what others have to say about your dreams and desires. Many of our friends would say just give up on this idea about having children and enjoy each other's company. It was always the ones who already had children. I recalled one of my husband's good friend's wives telling me I should divorce my husband and find a new man who wanted children as much as I did. Wow, crazy people in this world. I would cry out to God, "Please take this desire out of me, if it's not meant to be."

Several months had passed since the incident at the infertility office. I was lying on the couch, watching the Christian channel, when Benny Hinn came across my TV, confessing "Speak it and it shall be done." and Creflo Dollar impressed upon me to, "Look to the bible verse that states what you want and declare it." I was exhausted; I just came in from an all-nighter (a trip that started at 9:00 PM went from a destination on the east coast to a destination on the west coast, and then turned right around and came home around 7:30 AM). I fell fast asleep on the couch. My stepson was living with us and knew he would be leaving but, I could not move to check on him. I did not even hear him leave the house when he did. I was in a deep sleep the REM kind. I could see a baby boy; he was a big boy with blonde hair and the most beautiful smile. As I looked at the woman carrying the baby, I wondered, *is that me?* I realized that it was not me and that the woman carrying the baby was taller than me and had a scarf on her head; her smile was just as engaging as her pretty eyes. Just then, the door slammed and I jumped up quickly from my sleep. I had tears down my face and yet my heart was jumping for joy.

The next day I went to my bible study and told the ladies everything that happened. The ladies from my bible study had been praying for me for several years at this point, and knew how much I wanted a baby. Everyone had an idea of what they thought was happening regarding my dream. One suggested we were going to adopt while others believed, in the dream I was seeing my child. To be honest, I did not know what to think.

I took my bible with intent to find all of those verses of promises, and highlighted and wrote down any verse that had to do with pregnancy, or meant to encourage me. After covering the entire bible, I had three pages of verses that I had recorded and would say and read every night, over and over again. I would take these verses on trips with me and wherever I went, I would recite them and pray over them. This went on for many years!

I don't know what circumstances or trials you are facing but, as a new Believer, there is great hope in the

Word of God. I can share that I had no clue about the Bible; I only knew it gave me peace and knowledge every time I got into reading it. I would encourage you to try the same, and now you don't need to purchase a bible because you can access Bible apps online. I still like to hold the paper and turn the pages. The child in me enjoys highlighting in the Bible to help me remember verses.

> This will bring health to your body and nourishment to your bones.
>
> Proverbs 3:8

> All Scripture is God-breathed and is useful for teaching, rebuking, correcting and training in righteousness, so that the servant of God may be thoroughly equipped for every good work.
>
> 2Timothy 3:16-17

Case and point, I was having a difficult time with my husband, you know the kind where you stay on your side of the bed, to the point where you get a crease mark on your face by sleeping so close to the edge of the bed ensuring no body parts would touch, needless to say you get no sleep from your deep concentration or fear of moving.

You know that morning your spouse wakes up with a loud 'mm,' followed by a big stretch, with arms dangling like a monkey, you can't help but look, when you notice the big smile on his face with the comment, "I got the best night sleep." You on the other hand, can't wait for that first cup of coffee so that you can maybe identify the ground to which you're trying to stand on. With my feet dangling off the bed and full of contempt, I reached over for the Bible and said out loud, "Lord, give me a word." I closed my eyes, put the bible in my hand, and shoved my finger in the Bible. I know God can see that I am right. I open my eyes to verse:

> Love is patient and kind; it is not jealous or
> conceited or proud.
>
> 1 Corinthians 13:4

I let out a huff and say, "No!" I closed my eyes again and this time I asked, "Lord should I leave my husband?" As if the bible had now become one of those crazy eight ball's that you used as a child. After all, God is omnipresent (God sees everything, past, present, and future). The word my finger lands on is NO. Now I am mad as a hornet and say to myself, two out of three. I have now become defiant and a gambler. I shove my finger into the bible as if I am carrying a dagger. At this point, I can't even remember what the fight was all about only that I wanted to be justified. I opened my eyes and the word I landed on was NEVER the verse was:

> Keep your lives free from the love of money
> and be satisfied with what you have. For
> God has said, "I will never abandon you."
>
> Hebrews 13:5

Ouch, how does God do that? Not only did I realize I was justified but that my feelings were way off and the best part is that God has promised to be with me!

At the time, Delta was offering early-out packages to eliminate some of the senior staff. I told my husband let's do that, sell everything and sail all over the world. He smiled, and we actually began to make plans to make this a reality.

Although I thought how exciting it would be to do nothing but travel, the desire for a baby was still in me. My husband was getting ready to leave on a trip to Hawaii. He was in the bathroom with just a towel wrapped around his waist and shaving cream on his face. I confronted him that I wanted a baby still and he said, "I know but, I do not want to do infertility treatments anymore!" I tell him, neither do I. I believe God is going to give us a healthy baby. My husband smiled with a look of relief that came over his face.

I tell him that we both have to want to have this baby. He nods, and I tell him no, we both have to ask God right now for a baby. I insisted, "Let's get on our knees." We get down on our knees; our faces are looking out the window under the bathtub. I prayed to God for a baby and my husband and I then both say, "Amen."

I turn to my husband and prompt him, "Now, it's your turn!" My husband began to pray, and I try not to laugh because the shaving cream is falling down to his chest and every time he spoke his prayer, the cream plopped into the bathtub. He said, "Lord, please give us a healthy baby now; we are getting old in Jesus name!" We hugged each other, and he finished getting ready for his trip.

I spoke with my OB doctor early that week, who suggested I make an appointment with a radiologist, just to see if the damage was as bad as we expected. I think my doctor did this to 'shut me up once and for all.' As I signed in at the radiologist office, the receptionist directed me to the nurse for just a moment. I was told to have a seat and someone would be out shortly. This meant it was going to be a while, so I scan around for the latest magazine, the dates on them are old, normally, this wouldn't bother me, but then I began to notice that everything looked old and dated. The building looked old, the wallpaper was outdated, and the only thing new was the kid's bible on the table.

I picked it up and noticed the binding did not look like anyone had opened it yet. Just then, the nurse came into the lobby and sat right next to me; she smiled and said, "You must be Cindi."

"Yes," I said as I sat up straight to greet her.

"Are you a Christian?" she smiled and asked.

Still holding the bible in my hand, I nodded.

"Let's sit right here and talk since no else is here," she suggested.

I smiled my approval and she began to ask me all sorts of questions pertaining to my health. The nurse gave me an overview as to what to expect in the exam room.

I told her this was not my first rodeo and I shared with her all the miscarriages I had had thus far. The woman began to tear up and say how terribly sorry she was for me. I grabbed a tissue from my purse, opening it wide and she saw a glimpse of the bible I carry with me. She shared with me that the doctor has just become a Christian. I tell her my story and we both began to cry.

As I finished sharing, we both simultaneously proclaimed, "God is good, he has a good plan for our lives." We hugged and she left me with, "As soon as the doctor gets here, I will put you in an exam room right away."

After thirty minutes in the waiting room, I am finally taken back to the exam room where I meet the doctor. He carefully reviewed with me the procedure and added, "The nurse has told me your story."

"Likewise," I reply.

Then, to my surprise, the doctor suggested, "Let's pray before we begin."

I have to tell you that this is the first doctor who openly prayed for me since the beginning of my odyssey to get pregnant. The doctor called in the nurse. There I was, lying on the medical table, with nothing on except the green medical gown and, my Irish socks – the ones with the hole where my big toe sticks out, revealing my bubble gum pink nail polish.

The doctor encouraged us to, "Grab hands." We all do. It was the sweetest thing. He prays simply, "God, please help this woman conceive, and to have a healthy baby." I'm almost in tears that they should take time to pray for me, and it blessed me deeply.

The doctor then reviewed what to expect after the procedure, and emphasized that the best time to get pregnant is right after the procedure. He explained that he is going to blow my tubes open and remove anything in its way.

I kept quiet, mostly to hold back my tears of anger. As it turned out, wouldn't you know, this evening, my husband was on a trip and not expected back for another two days. The procedure was quick, and I was told some minor discomfort might occur, along with some bleeding. They were right, but I took some Tylenol and went to bed, and managed through it.

Shortly after I fell asleep, I heard my dog barking, followed by the sound of her paws clicking on the stairs as she was running down the steps. Surprise! My husband was unexpectedly home. He came into the bedroom and proceeded to tell me that they had a mechanical and had to cancel the last part of the scheduled trip. I smiled and told him all that happened. We would soon confirm what the doctor had stated to me in the exam room. That was the night we conceived our beloved son Jacob. We did not discover the pregnancy right away this time, though time would soon reveal the pregnancy.

"You should keep working," he smiled, perplexed. "You're going to be bored."

Chapter Fourteen

MIRACULOUS HEALINGS

I believe that God saved and supernaturally healed me on numerous occasions throughout my life. During one particular time, I noticed a lot of changes taking place, two things were especially bothersome - one was mood swings, the other was hot flashes. I called my doctor and explained my condition.

"With your age and family history, it's possible you are going through the changes," she seemed to know right away. "Come on in this week."

I made an appointment for that Thursday. The doctor took blood and urine and explained, I'm checking your levels now, just give me a few minutes. An hour goes by; at this point I'm thinking the worse, after all, why make me wait this long?

Every time I would see the nurse walk past the room, I would ask, "What's going on? Why is it taking so long?" The response was the same, "She is still testing." I'm thinking *this can't be good, it's got to be cancer*! The doctor finally came back in the room with a perplexed look on her face. I just blurt out, "It's cancer; just tell me, I can handle it!"

The doctor says "No! I didn't believe what I was seeing, so I got a different test kit and did the test four more times, getting the same result.

Then she said the most beautiful words ever, "You are pregnant!"

We both jumped up and down, and the nurses all screamed with me, in excitement. I think we went through an entire box of tissues."

The doctor does an exam and suggested we take a look using a sonogram. I go into the next room and the doctor was surprised, "Oh my goodness, Cindi, you are more than three months pregnant!"

She connected the fetal heart monitor, a device to hear the heartbeat, and, for the first time, I could hear the sound of my baby's heart beating loudly. What a beautiful sound! I want my husband to hear this beautiful sound, too. When I finished with my check up, I make another appointment for him to have the same experience when he returns from his flight.

I'm so excited, I hurry home. I want to call my mom. I no sooner pick up the phone to call and tell her, that I drop the phone and start thinking the worse. Instead, I pick up the phone and call my manager at work to tell her to pull my papers for my leave. Thank goodness they did not process them yet. I would keep my job and work a ground job. I still had not told anyone about the pregnancy, fearing the worse.

I remember asking God to comfort me, and every time I would open the bible, the same verse would pop up about Hanna wanting a baby. 1 Samuel 1-28.

In Samuel, the story of Hanna is told, a woman who also wanted to have a baby but, God had closed her womb. Hanna was the second wife, and the first wife of Elkanah would taunt poor Hanna about not having children. Hanna's husband had loved her more than the other wife and would offer to the Lord double portion for Hanna's sake. Hanna promised the Lord that if He would bless her with a son, she would honor Him.

My manager called me back and informed me that there were no openings for a ground position in In-Flight but, offers an opening in the Lost Baggage department.

"I'll take it," I said without hesitation.

I was placed in Lost Baggage, not the most ideal place to put hormonal pregnant women, but, it was an opening, and I had a higher priority. Who should I meet there?

The lady from my dreams who was wearing the scarf I saw in my dream. I later found out that she was a flight attendant, also on maternity transition assignment. She was single and her boyfriend wanted nothing to do with the baby. We became instant friends, and she even lived with me for a time, before and after her son was born.

During my pregnancy, my husband and I would be overcome with fear, understandably. I had finished reading Joyce Meyer's book, "Battlefield of the Mind," and heard her say the acronym for FEAR was defined as 'false evidence appearing real.' I kept believing something good, and replaced all the negative thoughts with positive thoughts. In spite of this intentional practice, I could not help myself feel overwhelmed at times.

Let's face it; the ratio of good to bad was not in my favor in regards to birthing a baby. I kept the scriptures next to my bed and read them every day and night. On one particular night, I had called my friend Lillian and told her about the fears I was having.

Lillian immediately prayed, "I pray that God will give you visions and dreams." I thanked her and got ready for bed that night. I was reading the bible and uplifted by this verse:

> I tell you the truth, you can say to this mountain, 'May you be lifted up and thrown into the sea,' and it will happen. But you must really believe it will happen and have no doubt in your heart.
>
> Mark 11:23

I asked God to reveal to me all truths. Oh, my goodness, this was the first time that I asked God and received it. That night, God showed me that we were going to have a healthy boy and that I could not doubt it.

I was now at my sixteenth week checkup when the nurse asked my husband and me when we wanted to schedule the amniocentesis.

"What's that?" my husband asked.

The nurse explained the procedure and how it is a predictor for Down syndrome in the baby; or, something along those lines, but that the information could be used to determine if we wanted to terminate the pregnancy, based on deformities.

"I'm not having that!" I said.

My husband thought differently, saying at our age we need to know ahead of time all the possibilities of what's going to happen. I told him, "There is the door." I'm not going to have any kind of procedure such as this. I told the nurse to explain to my husband the chances of miscarriage because of the test, she did. My husband still thought it was a good idea. I told him that, "I will never do that! I don't care what the test may results might be, I'm not changing my mind about the baby."

I told him what God had revealed to me about having a healthy baby boy. As usual, he just stood dumbfounded and said,"WOW.' On a side note, we did not know at this point we were having a boy. When we went in for our check up to find out the sex of the baby that is when my husband finally believed everything I had told him. I never allowed anyone to steal my peace or joy over this pregnancy ever, and, finally my husband agreed with me.

In late February, I gave birth to a healthy baby boy. Life was great! Delta Airlines was offering long term leaves because of the 9/11 incident. I took a five year leave and enjoyed my time as a new, older mommy. We did music together, joined MOPS (Mothers of Preschoolers), and read in the library. I loved everything about my life. My husband is a diehard Presbyterian and so I joined the bible study they offered. It was perfect. I would take my son to preschool and stay for Bible study with the women's group.

At the time, we were studying "Bad Girls of the Bible." During the study, I heard the Lord say to me, "You are making Jacob your Idol," and that I needed to be like Abraham, and "sacrifice Isaac." In my mind, I was hearing that I needed to give Jacob up. Remember, before I got pregnant I told God that if he gave me a child, I would honor Him. I never agreed that I would do what Hanna did and give my son to the priests. I just said, "I would honor you," I implored God for clarification. How could God ask me to do such a horrible thing after all I had been through, just to get to this point?

At my bible study class, I told the ladies what God said to me. Two of the women said, "I wish God would talk with me like that." Then another lady chimed in and asked, "But, would you want to go through everything she went through?" They both shook their heads emphatically, no. I never realized my life was so rough until then.

The same girl said, "God would never ask a woman to do that, you must have heard wrong." That night I did not want to read my bible or hear from God. I was so angry, that it took almost three years before I wanted to talk with God again.

Everything was going wrong in my life, the one night I watched Joyce Meyers and heard her say, "If you have a problem in your life, and God told you to do something, and you did not do it, you will never progress from that point."

At the time we were studying Priscilla Shirer's book of Jonah. In case you forgot the story of Jonah, he was to go to Nivea and tell the people how much they were sinning. What did Jonah do, but go in the opposite direction to Tarshis. Sound familiar?

I did not want to hear the truth, so I quit that mom's group and went to another mom's group, hoping to find something more to my liking to study.

I got the Jonah message and became very angry with God. "Why you would do this to me?" I would fret as I prayed and talked with God. "After everything I have been through, why would you take away my one joy, the only thing I ever wanted? What did I do that was so bad?"

Then I heard the Lord say to me, "Did I not provide the sacrifice needed for Isaac? "Don't you know how much I love you both? Do you think you can love like me? You have no idea the love I have for Jacob."

That is when God showed me how he sacrificed his one and only son for all of us. I can only respond with sobs of tears, "Yes Lord!" I agreed, "Jacob is yours, not mine." I remember holding Jacob up, crying, and thinking some sort of plague would come upon us for my waywardness. After all, I'm Jewish, and, this is exactly what happens when you are disobedient.

Just then, exact opposite happened, I thought I already loved my son but, I was wrong. Not only did my love increase for my son, but for those who I had never met. Whenever I was watching the news and would see a hardened criminal, my usual response was one of disdain. Then the Lord pressed me to look at people differently, and see them in the way He saw them. The Lord knew how much I loved children and said to me, "When you see a child, or baby, do you see such evils as a rapist, a murderer, or criminal?"

"Of course not," I said.

As I look at people, I no longer see them as adults, but as a small child. To extend more love to others, picture that when you encounter them, that they might not realize they are offending you. See them as a small child trying to get a glass of water or tying their shoes. The Lord asked of me, "When your child does something wrong do you stop loving them?"

"No," I feel uncomfortable having held previous offenses or judgments of others.

The Lord told me that he never stops loving any of his children, just in case you missed it - that message is for the entire world! Do you even know how much God loves each of us? God loves you, God loves you, God loves you!

After first being overwhelmed, I actually became angry, *why didn't I know about Jesus sooner?* Thinking my life would have been better if I had, as if I missed everything along the way, and I blamed God believing everything that had happened to me was his entire fault. I even gave him my list of everything he should have done for me. God was laughing at me - I could actually hear laughter.

After a few minutes went by God reminded me of when I was in elementary school. I think it was the third grade when my family had moved to Miami, FL. It was a great house. Everyone had their own bedroom and the greatest bonus was we had an in- ground swimming pool. It was awesome! My dad figured out a way to heat the pool during the winter months by using the dishwasher and the outdoor bathroom; he was full of bright ideas.

During the summer of my third grade, my sister and I were bored and decided to go swimming. We asked mom who, of course, went over the rules - no running; don't eat before you swim, and no jumping in the shallow end. "Yes, mom, "we said, and jumped into the pool.

My sister and I jumped in the pool and began to swim and play games. One of the games we played was 'who can jump into the pool the fastest.' My sister was at the deep end and I had just gotten out of the pool near the middle. I decided to turn right where I was and jump in to beat her. I saw that I was in the pool first. I tried to move my arms, but I could not move them. I tried to move my legs, but I could not.

I remembered that when I jumped into the water, I hit my chin super hard, in fact, it smacked the bottom of the pool. I could hear in my head, like the sound of a rip cord –the one that you would use in a kids' toy car, it is pulled through the top and off they go. I realized I could not use my arms and legs in any way, but saw that I could use my fingers easily.

I thought if I could just push myself by using my fingers at the bottom of the pool I can make it to the steps and get out. Everything was going great until my sister jumped in the pool and pushed me back further into the deep end. I started to panic and could not breathe. I was so mad at my sister – couldn't she see what I was doing?

That is when I heard voices telling me "don't panic, stay calm." I did; I was staying calm. Then the voice said, "What would happen if you die?"

My mom would be terribly sad.

The voice asked, "What would happen if you had to live in a wheelchair?"

Definitely not, my mom and dad would both be sad, and my grandparents could not live with that.

I hear my mom screaming at me, "Get out of the pool."

Apparently, my sister became concerned and got mom to come outside. I don't know how but, I walked out of the pool and nearly knocked my mother over getting out of the pool. My sister kept saying, "That was amazing. You were under the water for almost thirty minutes. You should do that again and I bet you could make a record." I, on the other hand, had never been so scared - and calm - my entire life.

I had forgotten that happened to me until that infamous conversation with Him. What struck me the hardest was that God was in my life, but I had not yet accepted Christ in my life. I found that to be truly amazing.

When I was in high school, I had made some truly bad choices, choices that could have hurt me permanently. The Lord reminded me of that conversation about where He was during those rough times. Again, I thought to myself, he was with me, and, yet, I was not a believer in Christ. God must really love me, to love me when I was yet to be saved.

> God shows his love for us in that while we
> were still sinners, Christ died for us.
>   Romans 5:8

The Lord showed me this verse but, at the time, it did not dawn on me that before I was even born God loved me and still called me by name.

> I have called you by name; you are mine!
>   Isaiah 42:1

God knew all the things I would do and say, and yet, he still wanted me, and on top of all that - HE LOVES ME!

The most recent miracle was just a few years ago. My son was in elementary school and I had gone in for the usual female visit. My OBGYN doctor asked "why didn't you come in last year?'

"I thought I did," I was equally puzzled.

"No," she said, "you must have forgotten to make an appointment." Starting next year, schedule your routine exam on your birthday, this way you won't forget," she recommended.

I thought now, that's a birthday gift you won't forget. Like everyone in the world, life got busy, and I forgot to schedule my exam. A postcard arrived in the mail to bring this to my attention. 'Happy Birthday, please schedule your annual exam, and, by the way, it's time for a mammogram to be scheduled, as well.' I called right away and told her thank you for the great birthday gift. In spite of my gift, unfortunately, I could not get in for another two months to redeem it.

I arrived for my annual exam, when I discovered that my radiologist had moved into the same building as my gynecologist, making it a convenient 'one stop shop.'

The nurse was very kind and very apologetic for the discomfort of the exam. She took the first picture and assessed the initial impressions with an audible and unsettling, "hmm."

"That does not sound good" I commented with trepidation.

The nurse immediately excused herself. I sorted through the 'what if's.'

Surely, there must be something wrong with the machine.

The nurse returned with a more somber demeanor. It looks like you have fatty tissue breast but, there is something over in this area that we are unsure about, and the radiologist wants me to do an additional x ray," then she added, "I must tell you, this will hurt."

"What, the first one didn't hurt?" I asked, not excited about this second test. "What do you mean?"

"We have to put a special attachment on the machine, kind of a large spatula with a box on top of it to flatten the breast down; it helps us get a clearer photo."

The nurse put the attachment on the machine and instructed me to, "take a deep breath in." All I can say is that I truly saw stars, and I screamed very loudly, in fact it sounded like a horror movie, and I certainly felt I was in one, too. I have no doubt my scream cleared out the entire reception area.

And, with that, the nurse instructed me to, "Wait here!"

Like I was going anywhere, I thought. I still could hear the ringing in my ears and the desire to vomit overwhelmed me.

In a few minutes, the nurse returned and said, "The radiologist wants to do an ultrasound on your breast to rule out anything."

"Where is the radiologist?" I demanded to speak to him. The nurse handed the phone to me and transferred me to the radiologist. "Where are you?" I demand of this medical expert who was holding my peace and my results in his hands.

'I'm on the golf course, and I am looking at your report," he answered with all sincerity.

"How is this possible," I asked.

"I can see all the images on my phone," he explained without concern. "I'm playing with Dr. so and so, the oncologist, and he also confirms that you need to have the ultrasound.'

I'm not going to argue with that, but find his professional office of choice peculiar for my circumstances. I agree to have the test.

"I'm very sorry to tell you but, we have made an appointment for you with the oncologist for Monday," the nurse informs me. "The doctors don't want you to wait, just in case action is required, and after all, you have a very young son."

Her remarks hurt almost as much as the machine and the procedures.

This was the last day of school for my son. Typically, this was a day of big celebrations to recognize the last day of school. I had already dropped off the cupcakes and gift for teachers. I had made a ton of water balloons the night before - another tradition for explosive fun, honoring his exit from another year of school.

This year, things would be different. I was carrying a heavy weight with me as I drive home to meet the school bus. I am shelf-shocked and scared, but I share with my husband as soon as I am home.

"I'm so sorry," he said, "Let's pray!" We pray together, and then, in the same breath, he said, "I hope it doesn't interfere with my senior golf Olympics."

I could have hit him or kicked him I wanted to lash out physically to expel my pain; but, I was overwhelmed with the sudden turn of events, and the simultaneous celebrations for the last day of school. I decided to call my friend, Lillian, who also immediately suggested we pray. It was very uplifting and hopeful, and, all I can do is promise to keep her posted.

Within a few minutes, Lillian calls again. "Cindi, I almost forgot my friend Zimara is in Atlanta right now."

"Who is Zimara?" I asked. She tells me Zimara is her friend, a faith healer from South America. I had offered her a buddy pass to fly to Zurich to see her daughter. I was grateful, but certain the flight was probably gone. Lillian told me she could not get on a flight, and was likely still in the airport. I was confident that I could not get to the airport and back home in time to catch the school bus. Lillian reassured me that I should reach out to Zimara. She provided her phone number and encouraged me to call her right away. Her flight was full, Lillian explained, but she said she had hoped to leave on the morning flight.

I called the number, and the person answering spoke only Portuguese. I placed a call to my cleaning lady who speaks four languages, but she did not answer her phone or respond to my text message. I called Lillian back and explained that I didn't think it was going to work for me to reach Zimara. It was almost 12:00 and the bus was expected to arrive at 2:35. Lillian tells me to sit tight while she places a call to Zimara.

Lillian called back and said that her friend was staying with a gate agent she just met last night. I know I don't have time to drive to the city and make it back before the school bus arrived. Lillian was not giving up so easily, "Just Google it; maybe there is a short cut." I Google search for the quickest route to the address, and to my amazement, the address of the gate agent was in the same city as me, and it is located only five minutes from my house.

I don't hesitate to make another call; I simply get into the car and drive to the gate agent's house, where I encounter a line of people waiting to see Zimara for healing prayer. I stood out in the crowd as the only gringo in line.

A lady walked up right away and asked, "Who are you?"

I tell her my name and she asked how I knew Zimara. I shared with honesty, that I didn't know her but, my friend Lillian who I formerly worked with at Pan Am, now together at Delta, did, and had shared this address.

The woman asked me what position I held at Pan Am. I told her I was a flight attendant and that Lillian and I used to commute from Miami together. Then she asked my name, and, puzzled, my maiden name, as well. Then, she started laughing, while I stood puzzled by her side.

"What is so funny," I asked, growing uncomfortable in this crowd where I knew no one.

She asked me if I was' that Jewish girl whom Lillian and Charles had been praying.' The lady proceeded to tell me she went to church with Lillian and Charles in Florida and knew all about me and my family; she wanted to know if my family and I had accepted Christ into our lives? I told her I had, but my family had not yet.

I began to tell her that my son's school bus would be arriving home soon and that I had never been to a faith healer, and wasn't really sure what to expect. Next thing I know, the woman pulled me to the head of the line. I felt guilty but, everyone seemed to be smiling, no doubt they had said something to them. I was afraid to ask. I entered the house, not sure what to do or where to go. I had never been to a faith healer but, I had been to a witch doctor in Africa, by accident, when I was in Dakar and had a headache needing aspirin. I assumed the guide was taking me to a drug store; clearly, I was in the wrong hut, when the man did not speak English and cut a chicken in half. I threw up on everyone and was asked to leave. I still had the headache. So, the idea of faith healer was somewhat alarming to me.

The lady who had brought me up to the front door, told me just to walk in when we arrived to the screened door. I walked in. not sure of what to expect. All of a sudden, this woman began speaking to me in Portuguese. I just smiled and requested,

"English, please."

Next thing I know, this young girl about 16 years old walked down the steps and asked what I was there for? I tell her the story about Lillian, not wanting to let her know what is really wrong with me, just in case this is all a bunch of nonsense. The young girl calls on Zimara.

This petite heavy-set woman with a round face and the warmest smile walks down the steps with a bible in her hand; the lady who brought me to the head of the line in now standing next to me. Zimara speaks with a sing-song voice, and tells me I harbor unforgiveness in my heart, and that I need to confess and ask for forgiveness. I was wondering if she was talking about my husband from just a moment ago or something else, something deeper. I begin to pray, and ask God to forgive me. She put her hand on my left breast and I screamed as I felt intense heat, like a hot poker going through me. It was very alarming, and I am freaking out, not sure what is going on. All of a sudden, I feel like I'm going to vomit and the young woman grabs a plastic Wal-Mart bag and offers tissues for me to use. Simultaneously, Zimara puts her hands on my abdomen. I am scared and over-whelmed by it all.

"I've had enough," I shouted in a shaky voice. I jump out of the chair she had me sitting in, and ran to my car. It was almost 2:00 pm.

I arrived home just in time to gather the water bal-loons and organize the other moms to greet the kids on their last day of school.

"Where have you been?" everyone was screaming at me at once.

I started delegating and the festivities go off without a hitch, never having to confess to anyone what had just transpired. The kids are water bombed with balloons, super soaked, and I'm super relieved to have it all over with. I fired up the grill and had everything all ready for the after school party. No one knew what happened just a few hours earlier, except for my husband.

Monday morning, I drive into downtown Atlanta to meet with the golf-playing radiologist/oncologist team. He had my chart ready, not at all ruffled by our golf course consultation. He informed me of the sample he would take during my exam.

They were just waiting for the nurse to come in the room to assist him. In the waiting, he retrieved my file, and said, 'That's odd!"

"What's odd?" I asked.

"They normally send us a CD and all the films from the original testing," he closed the folder, and seemed rather frustrated.

"No problem, we can just do another ultrasound so we don't have to have you reschedule and come back."

Here we go again, I thought, as I recalled how uncomfortable the first round of tests had been. The ultrasound didn't seem to hurt as much this go-round. The nurse walked me back to the exam room, and the doctor was inside already waiting for me.

"I want to show you something," the doctor said. He pulled up the films, viewable on the computer to both of us, and explained, "We normally use hard copies but, since we only have what the office sent us via email from your test just now, we will look together on here,"

Using a pen, he showed me the place where he planned to do a biopsy. I looked intently at the picture on his computer, unsure of what he was showing me. Then he switched images, "Now look at the ones we took today."

"I don't see the star fish, anymore," I exclaimed.

"Neither do I," the doctor agreed. He asked me if I had done anything and I shared the story of my faith healing encounter with Zimara. All he could say was, "Hmm, I don't believe this," as he listened, he kept staring intently at my films.

He placed a call to the radiologist, where I originally had the test performed. The radiologist, an Indian man, repeated the same thing, "I don't believe this."

"What does this mean," I asked.

"We need to retest you in a couple of days," he said, still in unbelief. "This time, I am sending you to the Breast Care Specialists of Atlanta.

At that appointment, the doctor confirmed what we had known since my last appointment. "I don't see anything. Come back in three months."

God is healer. Lillian was right. I needed to see her friend Zimara. And, Zimara was right, I had unforgiveness in my heart, and, it was eating away at my flesh. I am so grateful we kept pressing in, and that through faith, God healed me.

To be compliant, I went back for my follow-up appointment in three months time, and was told to return every six months for the next three years. I am happy to announce I now schedule an annual exam and all is well.

> But I will restore you to health and heal
> your wounds, declares the Lord.
> Jeremiah 30:17

Chapter Fifteen

STAIRCASE TO HEAVEN

People I know and love continuously ask, "If God is real, why doesn't he speak to me?" The other line I hear is that God was alive and well, back in the days of Abraham, Moses and David but, times are different, and he's not around here anymore!

I was no different; I had questioned the same thing in my own life. How could there be a God when all these horrible things happened to some good people - and to some who are not so good.

The questions were constant and similar, "Who can hear from God?" "How can such a person be alive?" "Doesn't the bible tell us that if you look upon God you will certainly die?'

> But you may not look directly at my face,
> for no one may see me and live."
>   Exodus 33:20

"So, tell me how it is possible not to look at God, yet hear from him."

Perhaps you even may doubt the existence of God at all. My parents had just recently retired and we were about to take a trip of a lifetime. They were going to sail around the world for thirty days. Because they were going to be away for so long they decided to visit my family before their voyage. My son had recently started playing t-ball and my parents wanted to see my son before they left for a month.

We were having such a good time during their visit. They enjoyed seeing their grandson play t-ball for the first time. My dad is the kind of guy who has every electronic gizmo and that day was no different. He had cameras and gadgets ready for the game, and filmed my son at his practice, even before the game, still two days away.

You never heard such laughing. The practice field was next to a train track and every time a train would go by the entire team would run to the fence and scream Thomas the Tank Engine. No one could entice them back to the field until the train left. One little boy was in the outfield, picking up flowers, and would run them over to his mother during quiet times on the field. All the parents and family members were laughing and, on the video, you can hear my dad repeatedly saying, "This is too adorable."

After practice, we all went for pizza, laughing and talking about everything that went on at the baseball field. After eating, my dad began to complain of indigestion. My dad has had several issues with his heart since I was in high school. At first, I thought it was indigestion because he did not act like he was in a great deal of pain.

"Dad just took five antacids and is not getting any relief," my mom expressed her concern. "Dad is not taking care of himself; he should have gone to the cardiologist before we left for our trip."

A unanimous decision was made to take dad to the hospital, in spite of his resistance. I dropped my son and husband off at home and drove dad and mom to the hospital. Within minutes, the doctor entered the waiting room, and exclaims, "Your dad is having a heart attack." There was a thorough conversation of his medical condition and a prescription for a blood thinner. We were all very concerned

As they began administering his first injection while he was still at the hospital, the nurse comes asked if dad ever had a concussion.

My mom shakes her head no, but I disagree. I remember that he has, when he was having a stent put in previously, and the monitor fell on his head, slicing it open and knocking him out. Although the doctor then said it was unconfirmed, because he was also sedated and unconscious at the time.

"Cin, don't you remember what your sister Jill said about me coming to Atlanta when I retired?" I had forgotten all about that. My sister had told my dad and me that she had a dream where both mom and dad had retired, and Dad had a heart attack and died in the hospital. Just then, panic came over both dad and I, and we both said to the nurse, "Stop."

'This medicine is going to kill me," Dad exclaimed.

The doctor walked in and suggested that we needed to complete the medicine in order for it to be effective. The doctor insists that we must finish the last round, but that we could fly home or go to downtown Atlanta and have the stent completed there.

Dad and I look relieved and agreed that he would prefer to go to his own doctor back in Florida. I remember my sister's old boyfriend owned a plane and could maybe offer help to get my dad back home. I called my sister. The man conveyed that he was attending a party and too inebriated to fly. It was after a11:00 PM, and no more flights were scheduled to Miami. My sisters, Jill and Lauren, call, and agree to fly in early morning.

At 11:30 that night, they bring my dad, with my mom, by ambulance to downtown Atlanta Piedmont Hospital. I follow behind in my car, though I am beyond exhausted. They got my dad into a room and the nurse tells us that only one person at time can be in his room. My mom and I take turns sitting with dad. Dad fell asleep and my mom does as well, in the chair. The nurse shows me a room filled with chairs and says I can rest in there.

There was a flurry of early morning activity with an obvious change of staff and nurses. I walk into my dad's room and announce, "I'm going home."

"I think I will go with you," Mom announces.

Dad looks mad at this news and calls her firmly by her name, "Linda." Mom snaps back from the lack of sleep and assured him, "We will be back first thing in the morning. "

The nurse came in as we were about to leave, and announced that dad is scheduled for 10:00 AM surgery to have a stent put in, and to please arrive at least one hour before. It's already 1:30 AM, and, we are both exhausted, but we both nod our heads in agreement.

Mom and I make the drive, a quick 25 minutes – never would we see that in Atlanta during a busy work day. We say our goodnights. I check in on my son, kiss him on his forehead, and tuck him in a little tighter before sliding into bed myself. My husband is snoring away. I closed my eyes and fell fast asleep. At 6:30 AM, the hospital called and announced, "You have thirty minutes to say goodbye before he passes."

I jumped out of bed, wake my mom, and urge her to get dressed quickly - dad is not doing good, and we need to leave now!

It is Friday morning and the traffic is thick. I'm trying to maneuver through downtown Atlanta during morning rush hour, and it's like pea soup. I see a police officer on the shoulder, and ask for help. His reply was for me to drive more carefully before I kill someone. I called my church and a few friends and asked for them to pray. I started speaking in tongues and begging God to save my dad. I feel a strong peace come over me and I say to my mom, "Everything is going to be alright."

"I don't think so!"my mom dismissed by optimism. All of a sudden, the car in front of me jams on his brakes. I slammed on mine, and my mom pleads with me to "Please slow down."

We get to the hospital in thirty- five minutes, which is record time for morning rush hour. I run into the hospital, but I'm stopped by a woman from the hospital, who asked us to wait where we were. My mom and I waited for an excruciating minute, and then were encouraged up, via the elevator, and to my dad's room.

The nurse attending to him, demanded, "Give us a minute."

It was another excruciating minute waiting to enter, but, when we did, my dad is sound asleep, purring away. My mom walked over to my dad and opened his eyes, where she sees only white. She lets out a groan. The nurse walked in and informs us the doctor is on his way.

The doctor walked in and announced that dad has had an aneurysm. We can try to do surgery, but it's less than a one percent chance he will survive. I am not ready to say goodbye. I tell my mom to do it; what else is there? The doctor informed us that if dad survived, he would be a vegetable the rest of his life. My mom and the doctor walked out of the room together. I grabbed my dad's hand and begged him to ask Jesus into his life. I began to sob and plead with dad to call upon Jesus and tell him that all will be well.

My mom walked back into the room with the doctor and announces, "We are not going to do the surgery."

"Why, not?" I cry out. "It could save him!"

The doctor proceeds to tells us that his dad had the same thing happen and he had to let him go, as well. I was madder than a hornet.

"If Jill were here, she would tell you to have the surgery!" My sister was a nurse. She would rally for the surgery, too.

We called my sister and told her what just happened, but, sadly, she agreed.

"The doctor is right," she said. "Dad would not want to live like that."

I thought that everyone had gone mad. In my opinion, there was still a chance for him to recover, and to live. *Why won't they take the chance; don't they know the God I serve?*

We were are all crying and sobbing to the point the nurse told us that we were upsetting the other patients. The hospital called in a Rabbi and a Pastor to talk to us. My sister's boyfriend's family, who lives in Atlanta, came into the room, too. Everyone was surrounding my father with love. We were all in shock, just a few weeks ago, we were all celebrating the Jewish feasts together.

I called my husband and told him to keep our young son home. "Keep him happy; he doesn't need to be here," I said.

My sister and Lauren arrive within an hour. Lauren is like my inherited sister. My family had practically adopted Lauren as part of the family. In fact, when dad had his first bypass, he would not be taken back to the operating table until Lauren was there. As soon as Lauren arrived my dad said, "Now all my girls are here; I can go for surgery."

We were all in shock, and my dad just looked like he was sleeping, and that nothing has happened. My dad lasted for three days, surrounded by his family, in Atlanta. But, it was not his heart that killed him!

As we were driving home I told my mom that I believed dad was in Heaven.

My mom's words hurt, "I don't know if there is a heaven."

It broke my heart to hear her say that, especially after everything.

My mom and I walked in the door and headed upstairs to take showers and, to regain our composure. My son Jacob came running into my room soon after, with my mom right behind him. He jumped into my mom's arms and gave each of us kisses. My son asked, "Where is my Papa?"

My mom began to cry and I tell my son that Papa is in the hospital.

With his hands on his hips, my sons said, "Mama, Papa was here last night. I repeated after him, incredulously, "He was?"

"Yes, he had on his blue NY cap, and he was going up the moving stairs and he told me to "be good kid, I'll see you later."

My mom nearly fell over and I knew, without a doubt, that dad was in heaven!

Chapter Sixteen

WHO AM I

After my encounter in Los Angeles with E.V. Hill, I decided to read the New Testament. That is when I began to ask God more specifically, "Who Am I?"

I always heard the same response, "Why do you need a name?"

I was confused as to my identity. "Am I Jewish or Christian?" I had not heard of the term 'Completed Jew' or 'Messianic' yet. To be honest, the thought of being called anything but Jewish bothered me greatly.

Then I heard the Lord reply, "Aren't I enough for you?"

"Yes, God, but when people ask me, "Who are you?" How should I respond?" I was having a conversation with God about my frustrations.

"Tell them you are a believer," he said to me.

I thought that sounded good, then the inevitable happened I was attending a community Bible Study and everyone was to give a little information to introduce themselves, so we all could be better acquainted with each other. I thought this would be perfect, 'just tell them you are a believer,' and then I would not get the looks and the several hundred questions that followed when I would say, "I'm Jewish," as I had in the past.

My husband would tell me not to tell everyone about the light, some folks might freak out. It took me years to tell others what I have shared with you. I feared being judged, criticized, and people expressing contempt.

I listened to everyone in the group and felt confident to say, "I am a Believer," instead of something else, that is, until it was my turn to speak - my nerves were slightly strain. I smiled and said the usual small chat, married with child, work, how long we have lived in the city, what my husband's church affiliation was practiced, how long we had been married, and I ended with, "I call myself a Believer."

The lady next to me said, "Ditto, I'm a Baptacostal Epsicacolic."

We all laugh; she has managed to include almost all denominations in her self-description, and added it only took her five husbands to get there. Then added, it has taken her over twenty years to find out who she was in Christ.

What she said hit home for me. I have been so overwhelmed with losing my identity as a Jew that my entire focus was on the name or title I would be called. This may be hard for those of you who were raised in the church, too. I never fit in any particular group, please know I was always felt welcomed but, I wasn't brought up in the church nor was my family.

What I am trying to say is that it's very hard for me to be called a Christian, not because of Jesus but, because of what has happened to the Jewish people by those who called themselves Christians. I lost many family members in the Holocaust and the stories of those who had survived tell how their Christian neighbors or co-workers did such appalling things. Anti-Semitism is very real and our history continuously plays this narrative.

When I lived in Israel, I had a neighbor who was a Holocaust survivor. She told the story of how she and her family felt more German than Jewish. I was puzzled, she went on to explain that she never went to Temple and that her father and mother never needed God because they were both college educated. Her mother worked at the University as a professor and her dad was in the military. She said her parents thought the government was more relevant and had more power and authority than God.

That was until the gestapo came to her door one evening and informed her that the entire family was being arrested. My neighbor said she was shocked, that she didn't even know they were Jewish. Both her parents kept, "We are more German than we are Jewish." The Gestapo didn't care, and they were all arrested and put into work camps.

In my mind it was an affront to be called anything else but Jewish. My husband and I had this discussion and he said, "I don't consider my religion to be my culture." I told him that's because he wasn't the chosen race. Being Jewish is more than just a religion; it was a way of life. Confused, and continuously searching as to where I fit in, I pressed in to the word of God ferociously. I came across a scripture that finally helped me understand who I was.

> [17] "Do not think that I have come to abolish the Law or the Prophets; I have not come to abolish them but to fulfill them. [18] For truly I tell you, until heaven and earth disappear, not the smallest letter, not the least stroke of a pen, will by any means disappear from the Law until everything is accomplished.
> Mathew 5:17-18

Jesus did not come to do away with the law, but fulfill it. If you look at the early church and apostles, you will see that Jesus preached in the Temple and the Holy mount of God. Jesus never separated himself from the law. The Pharisees, Romans and Gentiles continuously attacked Jesus as the Messiah.

While I was attending many different denominational churches, I could not help but feel the division of all these denominations. I never quite fit into any one particular group. I loved the people but, definitely had a hard time with the laws to which they created. It was very funny to me, here I was a Jew trying to fulfill all the laws, which was impossible and then listening to my church pew partners creating new ones - at times I wanted to say have you seen the original?

The desire to find out who Christ was and how I fit in consumed me. I began to read the bible all the time, when I would be in line waiting - it could be at the bank, at the grocery store, or while shopping. I would whip my bible out at any given time. I would highlight the verses and ask questions often.

When I say 'ask questions' this means if you were standing next to me I would ask you, "What do you think that means?" and, point to the verse and ponder some more. On a side note, I was living in New York and the responses were hilarious, scary, and, spot-on. You see, when I moved to Long Island after living in Flushing and then in New York City, which is predominately Jewish, I thought everyone on Long Island was Christian. You probably asked yourself how I came up with this; it's because the majority of people all wore crosses and I could see there were churches everywhere.

In my upbringing I knew how powerful God was, after all, every year we would do our Passover Seder and God was 'omnipresence and omnipotent.' These words illustrate how I felt about God, that he was everywhere, and the most powerful. Every year we would read how the Jewish people were the chosen children of God and how he rescued them from the taskmasters of Egypt. How God split the sea, and all the Israelites passed safely to the other side, while swallowing all the Egyptian army into the sea. Who could think of such things but a powerful God!

I soon realized God was showing me who Jesus was. When I began my journey, I was clueless as to whom I was in Christ. Let's face it, the only thing I knew about Jesus was from the movie The Grinch (the original), and the Charlie Brown Christmas movie. That was the only thing we were allowed to watch that was Christian. I did not go to church until my husband said we were going. We had been married already for years and had only attended a reform synagogue before that. Neither one of us pushed it but, I began seeking God. My sweet husband would always say, "That's a good question, I never thought about that," then he slapped me on my back and said, "tell me what you find out." I guess he knew if I could ask him, I could find the answers, too.

One of the greatest gifts was going to the Joyce Meyer's women's conference. I learned something so amazing, that God loves me and there is nothing that can separate me from God. I was told that God knew already about ALL my sins, not just the few I admitted, but ALL and he still called me his - Thank you JESUS!!!!!

I truly felt free from condemnation and then I learned how much he loved everyone, not just those who confessed Jesus but everyone - the saved and the unsaved. I came home with several books, tapes and everything else I could carry in my suitcase, just no gift of tongues from the Joyce Meyer's Womens conference.

I began reading "Battlefield of the Mind, Me and My Big Mouth" while listening to Joyce Meyer's every day on the radio, as I was going to work, and on my way home from work. I also listened to Dr. Charles Stanley. I had purchased praise music, CD's, books and bible resources to soak up during my hours of commuting.

The church we had attended did not offer a contemporary service. I was shocked that people were clapping and dancing in church while attending the Joyce Meyer conference. I remember one time my husband took me to his church in Mississippi and a woman raised her hand during service. I asked my husband what she was doing, and he explained that she didn't attend the church. "We don't do that," he said. "Why is she doing that?" I asked, "Does she have a question?"

The man sitting next to us nearly fell over laughing and later came up to us and told my husband, "I love your little Jewish wife." I was not sure if he was being condescending or truthful.

My husband said that she raised her hand because, "that's what those crazy Pentecostals do." I asked him where Pentecostals are from, to which my husband replied, "Same place as Elvis." It's a wonder I learned anything at all.

God was so good to me; he placed people in my path with great knowledge about Jesus. This one woman who worked the gates at Kennedy airport would say to me all the time, "You need to find out who you are in Christ."

She would press into my heart and say, 'You need to have the revelation of who you are in Christ." She would give me scriptures and hand me her bulletin from her church. I was like a sponge and soaked it all in.

I remember asking God all the time, "Who Am I?" and the response was always the same, "Believer." One of the hardest things to accept about Christ is do you

BELIEVE? It's great to say I am a blood-bought child of the Highest God. Greater is he in me than he is of the world, or when God says you are healed, that you are blessed both coming and going, that all your sins are forgiven, and I can do all things in Christ who strengthens me, but, do you believe what God says as to who you are?

One of the hardest things for me to realize was who I was and actually believed who the Bible says I am. My mind and my emotions were in battle with the word of God. Don't get me wrong, I loved all the bible verses about how much God loves me, it was the next sentence that followed that was so hard.

> You are a blood-bought child of the most
> high God for you were bought with a price.
> So glorify God in your body.
> 1 Corinthians 6:20

When I first saw this in the bible and heard others talk about this, I literally thought I needed to get my physical body into shape. It's vital to maintain a healthy diet and keep yourself physically strong but, here is the takeaway for me - I still needed to do something in order to be right.

One of the hardest lessons to learn was about my own imperfections and how God saw them. I'm not talking just my physical inadequacies but, those things I did (sins). I don't know about you but, I have this recording playing all the time in my head saying all the negative things that have happened or that I have done. Yes, I would cast them down and replace them with new ones but, it was a vicious cycle.

> [8] Finally, brothers and sisters, whatever
> is true, whatever is noble, whatever is
> right, whatever is pure, whatever is lovely,

> whatever is admirable—if anything is
> excellent or praiseworthy—think about
> such things.
>
> Philippians 4:8

The truth was I had no idea about Grace. I have no doubt that my ignorance was based on my own doing. Yes, we said grace at dinner and when it came to family, grace was always allotted. But, in my daily walk probably not; there goes that misinterpretation of the free gift, and I know how much God loves me and you. I was a doer of the word, this way I know that I have done what I am supposed to do; I have earned my keep. As many would say, I was a Martha, Martha, Martha.

It's hard for anyone to believe that they are righteous when they can see what is going on in their own lives. That was exactly how I felt. I understand that all the blessing goes to those who are righteous but, I did not fit into that narrative.

This was a hard concept for me to get. I kept trying not to fail and that might work for a while and then, I would try to pull up my boot straps and again it would work for a while and then came the crash. The feeling of guilt and condemnations haunted me. I understood how the Israelites kept going around the same mountain for forty years. I would beg God to help.

The moment came when I finally got the revelation of who I am in Christ. I just gave up and said to God, "I can't take this anymore. I am tired of being such a disappointment to you and to myself."

I went into bathroom, closed the door and began to sob. I truly was in the pit of despair.

In my bathroom, I keep the Bible that was given to my husband and me when we first married, and I began to read, hoping to calm myself down and perhaps get out of this pit. There it was in Romans.

Therefore, there is now no condemnation for those who are in Christ Jesus,

> **2** because through Christ Jesus the law of the Spirit, who gives life, has set you free from the law of sin and death. **3** For what the law was powerless to do because it was weakened by the flesh, God did by sending his own Son in the likeness of sinful flesh to be a sin offering. And so he condemned sin in the flesh, **4** in order that the righteous requirement of the law might be fully met in us, who do not live according to the flesh but according to the Spirit. **5** Those who live according to the flesh have their minds set on what the flesh desires; but those who live in accordance with the Spirit have their minds set on what the Spirit desires.
>
> Romans 8:1-5

So how can I be righteous and receive all these great blessings? I can't, but because it is no longer I who lives but, Christ in me, I am now and forever righteous. It's a hard concept to grasp when you screw up and believe me, no matter how hard you try, we all fail and fall short of the glory of God. However, you can be confident that God will never stop loving you, nor will he ever stop intervening in your life. So, put on your armor of God daily and BELIEVE who you are by God's standards.

Chapter Seventeen

BACK TO SQUARE ONE

One of the hardest lessons I learned as a Christian is not just trusting God but, resting in God. I was taught the importance of doing a good job and doing it well. Through hard work and dedication, along with good manners, you will go far in life.

I still can hear my grandmother say, "No matter how smart you are or how great you can do a particular task, good manners will get you a lot farther than any piece of paper.

This was proven to me when life began to turn in directions I never expected or could have imagined. I had been married over twenty plus years and I had a wonderful home, filled with many momentums that I had gathered when I traveled all over the world plus many great stories. I felt satisfied with how I looked, minus the ten plus pounds I have been trying to lose since 2008. I lived in a great neighborhood with some great neighbors and friends. I had the perfect van for our family and lifestyle. From the outside everything was perfect yet, on the inside, I was miserable.

How could a person who has it all be so discontent? The truth is that I had put myself first and that is where my focus stayed. For example, when someone said something to me that could be construed as negative, I had a choice to either believe them or believe what the bible says. The Bible says that we do not war against flesh and blood but of principalities and wickedness in high places.

If it was a stranger, a person I had never met, I did not become easily offended but, if it were family that was another story. After all, my family knows me best, or at least knows which buttons to push. There had been tension in the family, and like in many families, the tension can manifest itself in many different forms.

I learned this from watching Joyce Meyers on the TV, saying, "If you are miserable then stop focusing on yourself." She then went on to say the best thing to do is 'Do Good and Trust God.'

Wow, that seemed easy, Ha! That was the hardest thing to do. Let's face it, in our society it's all about me and what's in it for me. I knew my feelings were not valid and that this kind of thinking was insane. I did a review, "I have everything I need. I have a roof over my head; my family and I are healthy; we are in a good place financially; I am blessed to have so many wonderful things and people in my life and, yet, I still felt lonely. I was full of lack and just craving for something more but, did not know what that was for me.

I felt stupid when I confided to a Christian mentor friend of my situation, her response blew my mind. "Let me see if I understand you," she said. "First you have a husband who provides for you." I forgot her husband's hours at work were cut and that she was cleaning homes to supplement their income. I drove a great car, while my friend had to share a car with her husband. My son still lived at home while her children lived far from her. Truly, I had nothing to complain about.

I sigh, knowing I was not going to get any sympathy, and politely tell her she is right. I am very thankful for all the wonderful things I have both in and outside my home but, that did not change how I felt. After that encounter, I was feeling worse than before. I realized I needed to make some changes. You know the Nike ad line is "just do it!" I put a lot of zest in everything I did. I cleaned my house with such zeal, it bordered on OCD. I had hosted everything from Tupperware to missionaries.

There I was, doing good yet, still feeling miserable. *I must not be doing enough, I thought.* I joined the Martha's at church who provide food for people in need, who either have suffered a loss, injury or just needed a little help. I volunteered at a rescue shelter for dogs, which was great to see, but sad when others would not adopt. I helped at my son's school as room mom for three years, sold ice cream in the cafeteria for five years and volunteered at the school's library for four years, while still working full time as a flight attendant.

Like Joyce Meyer's said, the best way to get yourself off your mind is do for someone else. I did all these great things and felt good about it yet, I still felt like I was missing something. Why was this? Why could I not get happy or be satisfied? One night while reading the bible in the bathtub, my favorite quiet place, I discovered a truth.

The bathroom was my sanctuary, or as others would say, my war room. There is something about being so vulnerable and relaxed to hear more clearly what God is trying to say to you.

I cried out to God, is this it? If it is, this stinks! I flipped open the bible and there I began to read James 1:3 [3] You know that you learn to endure by having your faith tested.

My faith was being tested, only I did not realize what was happening. Like so many people I became very routine in my pursuit, almost to stagnation. I thought, *oh my goodness I'm just like the Israelites murmuring and complaining.* Remember how God had parted the Red Sea and they walked through on dry land. God provided a light for them to follow and sent manna from heaven for all to eat and never go hungry. The best part was that no one had to get clothes or shoes for forty years; they never once had damaged clothing or shoes. Think about the children, many were just infants when they left Egypt. Here I had experienced all the miraculous blessings in my own personal life, yet I was not satisfied, I wanted something more.

In the month of June, 2017, my husband was diagnosed with colon cancer and he was told not to delay in the surgery. As life would have it, this was also the time our beloved granddaughter was about to be born very prematurely. My mother came down after I was told that my husband needed a second operation because he had developed a staph infection, along with a kink in his intestine.

At this point, my husband was delusional and thought he was a pilot on a trip and I was the flight attendant. If I did not spend all day and night at the hospital, he would call screaming, demanding that I drop everything and get to the (hotel or airport), which was truly the hospital.

Our son had a job working at the club house at the pool snack shack nearby. He was hot and tired and had no clue as to what was happening with his father's changing behaviors. I kept my step sons informed of everything that was happening, while being mindful of all their responsibilities and how it would affect them.

I began to call everyone we knew to pray for my husband, and for my sanity. A good friend of mine came to the hospital and while her intentions were good unfortunately, it fell short of helpful. The night before my husband had a terrible night and became very confused as to where he was. The night nurse did not turn on his bed alarm and when my husband got up to use the rest room he became disoriented and was lost in the hospital. Needless to say, he had an accident and fell, and eventually he was able to make it back to his room. When I arrived at the hospital that morning, after much needed rest and a hot shower, I was greeted with the cold shoulder from my husband and the tech was still cleaning my husband up.

My husband told me all night he was left alone and could not find the bathroom and fell in the process of looking for it. He was very upset about the ordeal that had happened and said we should leave this hotel immediately. I looked at the tech and the tech replied that she had found him in the hallway.

I was enraged, that my husband was put in harm's way and treated with such disrespect. Here was a man who flew around the world, worked as a copilot on Airforce three and had been selected into NASA. I was outraged and upset with myself for not staying, believing if I had stayed, none of this would have happened. The hospital was on cover up mode when my friend walked in.

I immediately relayed everything that had transpired with my husband and how angry and upset I felt about the situation. My friend patiently waited for me to finish and then said, "Cin, you have a spirit of offense on you."

"I what?" this was no time, and I was taken aback at the statement. My friend said that she was also going through the same thing. She went on to say that no matter the circumstances you should not be offended. I plainly tell her I'm upset with the situation and how my husband was treated.

I asked her, "If this was your child would you not be upset?" "Of course, she agreed, but I would not be offended."

Just than the doctor walked in and asked me to fill out papers necessary for his impending operation. Right there, in the midst of all the confusion, I signed my husband's life away.

I am nauseous, mad, and exceedingly angrier. I let my husband know I was going home for a few minutes and check in on our son, my mom, and the dog.

"You have no food in the house," my mom informs me as soon as I walk in the door. "What's for dinner?"

I assured her I would pick something up, and I also offered the keys to my husband's car. I asked my son to take the dog for a walk, to which he replied, I can't." He defended his refusal and explained how he just walked in the door and was dying of heat. He asked if I could please walk the dog.

I thought it was probably the best thing for me, to walk the dog. I get the leash on the dog and began to walk him round our neighborhood. I'm now telling the dog everything that happened, and I look affectionately at my dog and say, sincerely, "Thank you God for my dog." I look up to the heavens and say, "I am ever so thankful to have a great dog." As I put my eyes back on my dog, there is my precious pooch rolling on some dead armadillo. My dog is now covered with blood and other parts of the armadillo and whoever and whatever was next to it, lying dead in the street.

This is when I lost it completely and screamed, "ARE YOU KIDDING ME?"

"You have my attention God, what is it?" I clearly am listening now. "Please tell me what is going on?" While scraping off my dog with sticks and leaves and gagging from the smells and sight, I am starting to sob and cry out to God, demanding an answer.

Just as the wind began to change direction, I could hear that still small voice asking, "Are you ready to let go now?"

I dropped the leash and raised my hands, as if I was carrying a platter and shouted, *"Take it all!"*

I was beyond 'put a fork in it' done. It was at 'drop the mic and call it quits' time. I was completely done, and, I completely surrendered it all.

I walked back to the house, opened the garage, and proceeded to clean my dog from the foul stench he had intentionally rolled into. My son and his friend met me at the garage door and began to tell me that when they got home from work, as they were pulling up the driveway, even before they entered the house, they could hear the TV blaring all the way from the mailbox. They both were laughing, and, we all knew it was my mom from watching the TV at a high volume. My son said that when he opened the door, the dog was barking, and the alarm went off with a loud siren, and my mom never moved from the couch, or flinched from the intrusion. When they approached my mom, she jumped and told them they were rotten kids for startling her.

"You should make more noise when you come in the house," she fussed like a grandmother would. They both were laughing, and I reminded them they would get old one day.

I entered the house and my mom informs me that she found the take-out menus in my catch-all drawer, and placed an order for dinner. I smiled with relief that, finally, someone had taken charge and help was on the way, even if it was simply dinner.

I told my mom what happened with the dog, and even how the boys had heard the TV at high volume;

we both laugh. I hugged my mom, grateful she was here, and that we could still share a laugh together. After our food arrived and we nearly devoured it, we headed back to the hospital.

As we came off the elevator, we bumped into one of my husband's golf buddies. He said he had just left the room, and then, he gave us something that helped him while he was going through cancer. I tell him 'Thank you' and how much we appreciate the visit. He told me how he and his wife were going to come by later in the week but, he said the Lord told him to come now. His comment was concerning, but I knew he meant well. We walked with more urgency to my husband's room.

My husband was reading what his friend had just given him. I was curious to learn what information it held. Inside a legal envelope, were Biblical scriptures with my husband's name, in lieu of original text - there were over fifty bible verses. Every day we would read them, and I would post them everywhere in his room. I would tape the verses every place he could see them. We both found great comfort and hope in every verse. I would place these verses on the mirror, taped to the curtains, laid on a table, taped to the back of chairs and posted like wallpaper on the walls. People would come in and also read them, the doctors, the nurses, the technicians, and even friends and family. These scriptures brought peace not just to us but, to those who entered the room.

I had been trying to figure things out and work them out to the best of my abilities and had some degree of success the problem was the other 99 percent I could not do or failed miserably in. My problem was my belief system (controller) was messed up. Sometimes it hard to believe there is a good plan when all around you is ciaos. You see I needed to understand that yes God knew already everything that was happening before it even happened; he just forgot to tell me, so I could handle it better. The truth is it is very rare to get the game plan before the game. I, we need to believe that before whatever you are asking, seeking, or needing you must believe before we ever see the manifestation is to trust God and know it is already finished and finished with excellence. Stop looking at the problem and trying to figure out the solution, just trust Jesus, the finished work, and REST.

Chapter Eighteen

THE COST

People often approach me after I speak and seem to ask the same question in regards helping a Jewish person accept Christ. The conversation usually starts like this: I have a friend or family member that is Jewish; what can I say or do to help that person accept Jesus as the Messiah? For the record, I would like to state that I am just one Jew of many who has accepted Christ as my Messiah, my EVERYTHING.

There is not one straight forward answer to this question. Several variables impact the answer and the path to salvation. The obvious factor is the law, in other words what does the bible say, according to the law of Jesus, as outlined in his Holy Word. The second is tradition, and the last is that we must ask, who gets to decide or, even, has God already decided?

If you were raised Jewish, you know that Jews don't believe that Jesus is the Messiah. I remember one time asking my parents why Jews don't believe in Jesus.

"The Rabbi said so," my mom replied. End of story. So many Jews feel the same way. If Jesus is the Messiah, then everyone would know. But what do the religious leaders of Judaism say?

According to many Chabad Rabbis, the Messiah is not identified by his ability to perform earth-shattering miracles. In fact, he isn't required to perform any miracles at all – although, the performance of miracles doesn't disqualify him either; miracles are simply not a defining factor. As written by the famous Polish Philosopher, Maimonides, a Sephardic Jew, who, during the medieval times defined the Messiah with specific, measurable criteria.

He instructed the Jews to be alert to the following: if we see a Jewish leader who (a) toils in the study of Torah and is meticulous about the observance of the mitzvoth, the collection of 613 commandments that are to be performed or avoided, and based on the Torah and the interpretations of the Sages; (b) influences the Jews to follow the ways of the Torah, and (c) wages the "battles of God"—such a person is the "presumptive Messiah."

If the person succeeded in all these endeavors, and then rebuilds the Holy Temple in Jerusalem, and facilitates the ingathering of the Jews to the Land of Israel— then we are certain that he is the Messiah, according to Maimonides, and accepted Jewish teaching.

When I first accepted Christ into my life, I must admit, I did not share with anyone that I became a Christian. I did this, not to deny my personal walk with my Lord and Savior but, that I was afraid to be judged by others, especially those in my family and still of the Jewish faith. Yes, even though I had the miraculous encounter with God, I was scared of my family, friends and, even, strangers. I did not want to be rejected or regarded as crazy for making such an extreme profession of faith.

As time passed and I began to seek, or let me state the obvious - God kept intervening in my life, I knew I could no longer keep my decision private, and it was to be made known and public to all. I was no different than the rest of you. I had many questions, like, why didn't Jesus get off the cross and show everyone he was God?

My dad would repeat this one to me all the time, to which I would reply, "Had he not died, we would never have the gift of the Holy Spirit."

My mom's favorite question reflected her view of authority,"If Jesus was the messiah, why didn't the head Rabbis say so?"

I thought this was rather ironic, especially since my mom always taught us to think for ourselves and not to be persuaded just because the crowds think one way. As I am sure you have heard, 'If it quacks like a duck and has feathers, do you call it a car?' This might sound better in Yiddish than English but, you get the gist of it.

To enlighten you more about a Jewish perspective, besides my family, here are just a few thoughts that I have heard over time. If you want to get a Jewish perspective of any subject, just ask one and you will have three different ideas by the end of the conversation. For example, when asking a Jewish person on any subject that is either intra-perspective or direct on any subject, not only will they give their own opinion of the subject, they will give you their friends idea, their parent's perspective, and their deceased grandparents thoughts on the subject - and all of them would most definitely hold very different ideas, regardless of whether it's for simple directions or making a meal.

After my trip to Brussels, God revealed himself to me yet again. This time the Lord reminded me of all the times he was there beside me. I was not saved during the times he showed me, nor did I have any intentions of being a Christian and saved. The Lord showed me how he was with me when I was a young person swimming in our home pool, when he miraculously showed up at the right time even though I thought it was the end of my life.

Then there was the time I was driving in a car and may have had a little too much to drink. God was beside me. And, when I had lost our baby boy, there was God, beside me again. The Lord showed me how he was with me in the worst of times in my life, through poor decisions of my own, and with those who made poor decisions, that ultimately harmed me, as well. The Lord reminded me that he was omnipresence which means basically God was everywhere all the time, in these times he showed me, and every other one, too.

"Do not be discouraged for the Lord your God will be with you wherever you go."
Joshua 1:9

What I didn't realize was how much God loved me for me - just as I am.

After that encounter in Brussels, God kept telling me to tell everyone, how much He Loves EVERYONE!!!!!

Whatever name you want to call yourself, whatever group you are affiliated with, all those labels you place on yourself or those others place on you, - they mean nothing to God.

"We love because God first loved us."
1 John 4:19

According to this scripture, you did nothing to deserve God's love. I always think of my son when I read this verse. Perhaps you are like me, when you always wanted children, and you were pregnant, and you loved what was being formed inside of you, and when your child arrived, you never knew you could love anyone or anything as much as you loved your child. That is how God feels about you - only greater!

> Lord, you have examined me and you
> know me. You know everything I do; from
> far away, you understand all my thoughts.
> Psalm 139 1-16

We are talking about those times and places that you think no one is looking or can hear you. Just imagine when you are thinking of things that you would not want anyone to hear but, instead they are playing over a loud-speaker, this is exactly how God hears you. **3** You see me, whether I am working or resting; you know all my actions. 4 Even before I speak, you already know what I will say. When I read this verse, it was mind blowing to think that even before we are born or thought of, God already knew what we were going to say and to whom we were going to say it.

When you read the first four verses, you see that God is all around us, this includes in both good times, and in times of troubles, whether caused by us or someone else. Just imagine that God knows our thoughts and deeds even before we think or do them, and yet, God is still calling us to press into Him.

I understand that some people like to blame God for all of their problems. Let's face it, if you never knew or heard from God, he can't argue with you, or conversely, tell you that He Loves You!

When you continue to read the Bible, you will gain a deeper understanding.

> You are all around me on every side;
> you protect me with your power. **6** Your
> knowledge of me is too deep; it is beyond

my understanding. **7** Where could I go to escape from you? Where could I get away from your presence? **8** If I went up to heaven, you would be there; if I lay down in the world of the dead, you would be there. **9** If I flew away beyond the east or lived in the farthest place in the west, **10** you would be there to lead me; you would be there to help me. **11** I could ask the darkness to hide me   or the light around me to turn into night, **12** but even darkness is not dark for you, and the night is as bright as the day. Darkness and light are the same to you. **13** You created every part of me; you put me together in my mother's womb. **14** I praise you because you are to be feared; all you do is strange and wonderful. I know it with all my heart. **15** When my bones were being formed, carefully put together in my mother's womb, when I was growing there in secret, you knew that I was there.**16** You saw me before I was born. The days allotted to me had all been recorded in your book, before any of them ever began.

Psalm 139:5-16

I don't know about you but, this Psalm explains that before we were even thought of, God already knew us and wanted us. This includes everything, not just the things we tell people but, those things that are kept in the dark places that we share with only a few, or no one at all. The best part of God's promise is that God's love never changes NO Matter What We do.

Look back on verse ten for just a moment, **10** you would be there to lead me, you would be there to help me.

I can sincerely say YES, I have seen this in my own life, and I know that I know he is doing the same in your life, too. When God began to show me how much he loves all of us, he also gave me a hunger and a desire to read the bible more. As I began to read, I learned more and more about God, and that hunger intensified when I read scriptures. I must admit that I needed a dictionary to look up many of the words I did not understand, let alone the context of verse.

Every question I had, The Lord would show me in the Bible the meaning behind the things I was reading. One such time was when I had made a mistake, or sin for those who are hung up on semantics, and he gently corrected me. I know what I did was wrong and I began to feel this intense heaviness on my heart - the kind of heaviness you can visibly see when your child has done something wrong and, is too ashamed to admit he did wrong. The child begins avoids eye contact or look the other way. You can see in his face his inner anguish, and you are moved as a parent to try to help that child, by trying to coach him to speak about the situation, or perhaps you avoid direct acknowledgment, too, but, lay your hand on top of his head to give him some love. This is exactly how God feels about all of us when we miss the mark.

When I first began my Christian walk, or should I say my crawl, I thought many times that I was not worthy or fit to have all my sins removed especially since, after accepting Christ, I still sinned. I thought I blew it, no more 'Get out Hell' for me but, then something amazing happened. That freed me from this skewed thinking - God began to work on me and show me things I never thought about.

One such time was when I had judged someone rather harshly, and consequently it showed in my actions towards that person. Immediately I felt that heaviness on my heart but, I intentionally ignored those feelings and thoughts. I kept busy because I did not want to think about it, and when pressed to ignore them, did some retail therapy, instead. Needless to say, I was miserable, and I began to boohoo to friends and family, and finally to God. Please don't laugh at me but, as a baby Christian, I would take the Bible and say God, "Show me," and put my finger on a random verse in the Bible - and Low and behold, the answer was right there.

Such was the case in this instance. My finger fell right on Genesis - it was about the very first sin committed by Adam and Eve.

> "That evening they heard the Lord God walking in the garden, and they hid from him among the trees. **9** But the Lord God called out to the man, "Where are you?" **10** He answered, "I heard you in the garden; I was afraid and hid from you, because I was naked." **11** "Who told you that you were naked?" God asked. "Did you eat the fruit that I told you not to eat?"
>
> Genesis 3:8-11

This is where so many people, especially Christians, miss the mark. I will never forget when I was in a Bible study, and the leader of the study began to say that when we are sinning God cannot come near us, and all the people in the bible study were agreeing, and even giving scriptures to back this up. I don't know what came over me but, I said, "How that can be true if the Bible says in Romans, that,

> "**8** there is no condemnation now for those who live in union with Christ Jesus. **2** For

the law of the Spirit, which brings us life
in union with Christ Jesus, has set me free
from the law of sin and death.

Romans 8:1-2

The Leader agreed that this was true. We all sin
and therefore, God cannot come near us, because God
does not sin, he explained. At that moment I thought to
myself, *they are trying to justify themselves.* They have now
removed Jesus from the equation.

"If that were true," I challenged the leader, who became
a Christian later in life like me, "how then could you be a
Christian? You were a sinner when you accepted Christ
and, we all sin still. Does that mean God is not with you?"

The leader proceeded to say that he was a sinner when
he accepted Christ and yes, he still has sin in his life. I
asked him to clarify his teaching.

"How you can say God is not with you when you sin.
When you just said you accepted Christ while you were
still a sinner?"

As a Jew who loves the law, a part of me also under-
stands, it's impossible to fulfill all the laws that God
requires. Yes, I am a good person but, there is nothing
written in the scriptures that backs that up, that if you are
a 'good person,' God will overlook this or that. Because,
then, we would no longer need God, since we have
decided or judged what is good and evil - sound familiar,
as in Adam and Eve?

Here was my 'aha moment' about all of this. God
hates sin, but loves the sinner. His love is eternal and no
matter what we say, what we do, or how we do it, has
no bearing on how much God loves each of us. His Love
will never, ever change. In other words, there is nothing
that you can say or do to make God love you any more
than he already does. God's love is constant.

Give thanks to the Lord, because he is good;
his love is eternal. 2 Give thanks to the
greatest of all Gods; his love is eternal.

Psalm 136:1-2

This is one of my favorite verses, especially when I know I have missed the mark and perhaps, hurt someone or myself. This can be hard for some people to grasp because they might not have had anyone to show them that goodness, kindness and most importantly that kind of Love. But, here is the good news - God is the only one who can show and demonstrate that Love, and best of all, we will then be able to express that kind of Love to others through the Holy Spirit. Thanks to Jesus Christ, who gave us the Holy Spirit through his death on the cross at Calvary, and most importantly of all - the Holy Father who created all this from the very beginning.

You see, at this point in my life, I believed that Jesus was real but, I doubted who I was in Christ; I did not know who I was in Christ. When you accept Jesus Christ in your life, it's like a "Get out of Jail" card but, no clue as to what it means to be a follower of Jesus Christ. I had accepted salvation but, I was still in need of discipleship.

I think this would best be explained when I had my son Jacob. As you read before, my husband and I suffered through many miscarriages, and many doctors from the IVF community had informed us that there was nothing more they could do, and to simply accept our infertility.

Had my husband and I not moved to Atlanta, turned to TBN, or encountered the teachings of powerful leaders, such as: Creflo Dollar, Joyce Meyer, and Benny Hinn, to name a few, I wouldn't be here writing this book telling you of the many miraculous things God has done. When I began to watch that day, something powerful happened that stirred in me a hope and a desire to search the

164

scriptures, to find everything I could that would enable me to become pregnant and to never waiver in believing what God had put on my heart.

As you know, the miraculous happened, with the birth of our son Jacob. No sooner did my excitement then turn to grief when I heard the Lord say to me that I had made Jacob an idol, and that I needed to give Jacob up to God.

I am no Hannah; I never agreed that I would give Jacob up to the Lord. But, the Lord pressed in to me that I am to be like Abraham and offer Jacob up. I turned off the volume of God for three full years, and did not want to hear another thing from God.

When God did not give up on me in those years of silence, but kept pursuing me with the people he put on my path, and those people I never knew, who planted seeds in me, I realized he was faithful, and, he loved me for all eternity. I knew I still needed God when my life again became complicated.

"How dare you ask me to give up my son and offer him up to you?" I was rightfully angry when I did approach God again. God was just laughing at me from heaven.

"You think Jacob is yours?"

"Of course, he is," I adamantly justified my rights. "I take care of him in every way, and I feed him, clothe him, put a roof over his head, take him to the doctor and most importantly love on him always!"

God stood His ground and reminded me of a few things.

"Who do you think gives you all those skills, provisions, and commodities to provide for Jacob?"

That one was easy. My husband and I both had jobs. We sacrificed and worked long hours.

" I did, and my husband - we work to provide for Jacob!" I retorted boldly.

"And, who gives you your jobs and opportunities?"

"We do through our education and the choices that we made," I was equally stubborn to reply.

"No," God said, now with a gentler, soothing tone, "I am the creator of all things. Do you not know how much I love you and how much I love Jacob? With the same amount of love, I love you all. And tell me, can you part the sea? Can you put the stars in place, can you heal the sick?"

"No, of course not," I said more humbly than when I had began, "only you can do such things."

"Yet, you feel more qualified than *me* to care for your son. The truth is you do not trust me."

"You are right," I conceded, "but look what has happened in the past! How can I trust you when I have lost so much already?"

"What kind of God do you think I am? I have never asked you to sacrifice any child! I Love You and Jacob very much and only want good things for each of you. Yet ,you are the one who left me. You do not want to hear from me. You stopped reading the Bible – my precious Word. And yes, you still attend church and attend a Bible study, but with a lukewarm heart; you do not want to hear from me for fear that I will ask something of you that you do not like or want to do."

God was right, I was more afraid of what I created in my mind - the "what if's" I feared. Not to mention, I had to work through the feelings that came along with those fears. This is when God revealed to me more about trust. Do I trust God that he will help me and protect me, and most importantly, not judge me the way I would judge? The verse that God kept showing me was Proverbs 3:5-6.

"**5** Trust in the LORD with all your heart and lean not on your own understanding; **6** in

166

all your ways submit to him, and he will
make your paths straight.

Proverbs 3:5-6

How can I trust in God when all these horrible things
have happened to me? I would ask myself over and over.

This is when God revealed to me his confirmation in
Jeremiah.

I alone know the plans I have for you, plans to bring
you prosperity and not disaster, plans to bring about the
future you hope for. Jeremiah 29:11

I no longer needed to strive to get those things that I
wanted or needed. In fact, God had attended to it all.

You see, one of the greatest lessons in life I learned was
from Joyce Meyer's book, "Battlefield of the Mind." Her
book showed me that I needed to change my mind-set.
Until I had read her book, I focused on all negative things
and thoughts, and like most people, when I can't explain
something -whether good or bad, I blamed God. Once I
started to find out the true nature of God, and dismissed
those false thoughts and images I had created, my hope
intensified my love for others, who I would not normally
care for or be able to love. I was able to see them in a positive light again, my love intensified and, I was also able
to forgive again.

Like many of you, I had been hurt by those I loved.
Perhaps, you have been wronged by someone, too, more
often than not, that person had no clue they even hurt
you. The good news is that with Jesus, you can let it go.
You know the saying, "Let go and let God." Well, it's true.

You no longer need to protect yourself, or lash out,
or seek vengeance, because, the Lord is your vindicator.
This absolves you of having to play judge and jury. Now,
you can let God battle for you.

Just like Dr. E.V.Hill said to me that day at McDonalds, "Stand back. Call on Jesus, let it go, and watch God take care of it for you."

So whatever life has dealt you, just call upon Jesus and watch your deliverer take care of you. For we are not fighting against human beings, but against the wicked spiritual forces in the heavenly world, the rulers, authorities, and cosmic powers of this Dark Age. Ephesians 6:12

If you are reading this book I don't believe this was by chance but, a divine appointment designed by God just for you. Please take a moment and ask yourself, "Do I want to live with God and have a personal relationship with Him and be called friend of Jesus?"

If you said yes to this, simply say, "Jesus, come into my heart; I believe in you."

If you said that, get a bible and begin your journey. God will reveal to you all truths. Tell a friend and share with others what you have learned. Just remember this, God loves you - repeat after me, GOD LOVES ME! There is nothing that can separate you from God's Love. If I don't have the opportunity to meet you here on earth, I look forward to seeing you in Heaven.

Blessings,
Cindi

DO YOU KNOW HOW MUCH GOD LOVES YOU?

God loves you so much. I have heard Him say this over and over again. Tell them how much I love them.

And, when in doubt, He gave us a book full of promises to read over and over again.

Here are a few Bible verses that I read when I was trying to conceive:

> Isaac prayed to the LORD on behalf of his wife, because she was childless. The LORD answered his prayer, and his wife Rebekah became pregnant.
>
> Genesis 25:21

> Hannah was in deep anguish, crying bitterly as she prayed to the LORD. [11] And she made this vow: "O LORD of Heaven's Armies, if you will look upon my sorrow and answers my prayer and gives me a son, and then I will give him back to you. He will be yours for his entire lifetime, and as a sign that he has been dedicated to the LORD.
>
> 1Samuel 1:10-11

I tell you the truth, you can say to this mountain, 'May you be lifted up and thrown into the sea,' and it will happen, but you must really believe it will happen and have no doubt in your heart.

MARK 11:23

Take delight in the LORD, and he will give you your heart's desires.

Psalm 37:4

But those who hope in the LORD will renew their strength. They will soar on wings like eagles; they will run and not grow weary, they will walk and not be faint.

Isaiah 40:31

Jesus looked at them and said, "With man this is impossible, but with God all things are possible."

Mathew 19:26

I have told you these things so you may have peace in me. In the world you will have much trouble. But take hope! I have power over the world!

John 16:33

But you belong to God, my dear children. You have already won a victory over those people, because the Spirit who lives in you is greater than the spirit who lives in the world.

1John 4:4

Even though I walk through the darkest valley, I will fear no evil, for you are with me; your rod and your staff, they comfort me.

Psalm 23:4

Believe in the Lord Jesus, and you will be saved—you and your household.

Acts 16:31

"You are my witnesses," declares the LORD, "and my servant whom I have chosen, so that you may know and believe me and understand that I am he.

Isaiah 43:10

I can do all this through him who gives me strength.

Philippians 4:13

Even though I walk through the valley of the shadow of death, I will fear no evil, for you are with me; your rod and your staff, they comfort me.

Psalm 23:4

For God so loved the world that he gave his one and only Son, that whoever believes in him shall not perish but have eternal life.

John 3:16

Don't be afraid, for I am with you. Don't be discouraged, for I am your God. I will strengthen you and help you. I will hold you up with my victorious right hand.

Isaiah 41:10

I hope these verses encourage you always and strengthen you in your journey, as they have for me. These are some of my favorite verses. I hope you dig in to the Holy Bible and find your favorites, too.

-Cindi

CALL FOR SALVATION

Profess Jesus as your savior.

> "For whosoever shall call upon the name of
> the Lord shall be saved."
>
> Romans, 10:13

When your heart is ready, pray, "Father in Heaven, I believe that Jesus died for my sins. "I repent of my sins. Forgive me. I receive your free gift of salvation. Come into my heart."

And, God will impart eternal life to your spirit. It's that simple. No amount of sin can keep you from it. No amount of works or striving, no amount of miles you have run away can keep you from His free gift of love.

Jesus, the resurrected one, has the power to overcome death, to cover, forgive and save us from our sins. Just ask, as simple as the prayer above, or words straight from your heart, and He will forgive your sins. You will be His; no longer an orphan, but under the sonship of the risen Lord.

He will direct you to leave your 'life of sin and sin no more,' instead, walking out your life from a position of one forgiven, and one who loves others freely, as you have now first been forgiven, and loved.

He wants you to show forgiveness, love, and kindness to others, and to love Him,

> "With all your might, and all your soul, and all your strength."
>
> Mark 12:30

> Honor the Lord in all your ways and He will direct your paths.
>
> Proverbs 3:6

Lastly, believe in the Lord, because having faith in Him does 'work,' and yields a fruitful life.

> For it is by grace you have been saved, through faith—and this is not from your-selves, it is the gift of God— not by works, so that no one can boast.
>
> Ephesians 2:8-9

> For God so loved the world that he gave his one and only Son, that whoever believes in him shall not perish but have eternal life.
>
> John 3:16

God loves you, my friend.

God gave His only begotten son, because He loves both the saved, and unsaved, both you, and me.

You are loved.

CINDI MCCANN, AUTHOR

My name is Cindi McCann. My heart is to share with the world how God loves both the saved and the unsaved. I was born into the Jewish faith; it was my identity, until Jesus showed up and changed my life. Before I was an author, I was a flight attendant, and lived in several places, including Tel Aviv. I was born in Chicago, IL. I was raised in Miami, FL. I was graduated from Miami Killian Sr. High. I attended Tel Aviv University in Israel, and graduated from Miami Dade Community College and Point University. My degrees are in Counseling and Human Services with a Minor in Biblical Studies.

I began my career with Pan Am in the early 80's as a Flight Attendant. I was based in New York, Miami and London. During my career with Pan Am I was a purser, Language of destination speaker for English, Hebrew, French and Spanish. I also was a recruiter and Instructor for In Flight Service. In 1991-2008 I was hired with Delta Airlines as a Flight Attendant. I became an Operational Supervisor in 1995-1998 for LaGuardia Airport and JFK Airport. In 1998 I worked as a Human Resource Supervisor For In- Flight with a group of 260 personnel from all diverse backgrounds and country of origin at JFK Airport. In 1999 I was transferred to Atlanta as an In- Flight HR Supervisor for International, working with New Hires and Company transfers. I had the privilege working for Swiss Air in the exchange program with Delta in 2005-2006. I took an early out package and retired in 2008.

I am married to Tom McCann for 24 years. Together, we have one terrific son named Jacob, and we are also blessed with two equally outstanding step-sons who have just as wonderful wives. The newest addition to our family is GG, our sweet little granddaughter. We also enjoy our four-legged family member – our loveable mutt, Jack.

I accepted Jesus into my life in November, 1991 and have enjoyed the journey of life that God has designed for me. I deepen my faith and share the journey with others as a Bible Study teacher for my Church. And, her I share some of my favorite life quotes:

"From your mouth to God's ears."
"Alevei! - It should happen to me (to you)!"
"If God wanted me to have it, I'd have it."
-Cindi McCann, Author

CPSIA information can be obtained
at www.ICGtesting.com
Printed in the USA
FSHW02n2246230918

9 781545 628034